Journey with Jesus

April 25, 2017
St. Mark

Journey with Jesus

Encountering Christ in his Birth, Baptism,
Death, and Resurrection

Neil —.

With respect & affection,

C. FRANKLIN BROOKHART JR.

' Frank

RESOURCE *Publications* · Eugene, Oregon

JOURNEY WITH JESUS
Encountering Christ in his Birth, Baptism, Death, and Resurrection

Resource Publications
An Imprint of Wipf and Stock Publishers
199 W. 8th Ave., Suite 3
Eugene, OR 97401

www.wipfandstock.com

PAPERBACK ISBN: 978-1-4982-8073-0
HARDCOVER ISBN: 978-1-4982-8075-4
EBOOK ISBN: 978-1-4982-8074-7

Manufactured in the U.S.A.   NOVEMBER 14, 2016

Contents

Acknowledgments

I AM GRATEFUL TO General Theological Seminary and its Dean and President, the Very Rev. Kurt H. Dunkle, for graciously providing accommodations during the research stage of this book. Dean Dunkle opened the Christoph Keller Jr. Library for my use, and there I was ably assisted by the Rev. Andrew G. Kadel, Librarian, and Ms. Mary Robison, Reference Librarian.

I thank my wife Susan for encouraging me to write and providing an inspiring example. She generously offered time for me to work on this book. I am always grateful to her.

Introduction

I INVITE YOU TO go on an odyssey with me.

As with all journeys the first question is: what is our destination. Where exactly are we going? Our destination is simply Jesus Christ. We are on our trip in order to meet him. I am writing this introduction during the Great Fifty Days of Easter, and I have been struck by how often in the appointed scripture readings Jesus says, "Peace be with you." This is exactly the Jesus we want to encounter, the Risen One who gives us the gift of peace, shalom, all that we need to live in the way God intends for us.

But there is more. Not only do we want to hear Jesus greet us, but we also want to receive the gift of divine peace. We seek to find a way to make his gift a part of who we are. Our destination is to live at a deeper, transformed, resurrectional level, bathed in the life and love of God, which Jesus himself mediates to us. Our goal is to live in Christ as Christ lives in us.

That represents our destination. But how do we get there? By what means will we be able to make his journey? The answer is straightforward. We seek to find and be found by Christ by exploring the gospel story of Jesus. I propose to do that in a rather unique way. We will examine and contemplate the four signal events of Jesus' life.

We normally hear the gospel story in snippets read in church. I am not criticizing our use of the Bible in liturgy; indeed, I can think of no other way of dealing with scripture in worship other than by reading selected portions. But this does have the effect of preventing us from experiencing the sweep of the gospel. Furthermore, many people use devotional materials or study guides that either use the snippet approach or focus attention of the sayings of Jesus.

I believe there is another powerful mode of examining the gospel story. I propose that we seek to encounter Jesus by considering the four major events in his life: his incarnation, his baptism, his crucifixion, and his resurrection. They constitute the events that support both the story and its meanings.

We do not, however, stop there. After looking at each of these events we will appraise the possible ways in which Jesus' story intersects our story. Part of what makes scripture so important for us is that has many points of connection and attachment to our personal stories and to the stories of the churches of which we are a part. That is part of the reason we experience scripture as "holy."

In this manner, I believe Christ and the peace he offers will become our peace, and his story will become our story.

The chapters that follow should be seen as pairs. The first part will probe one of the four major events. I hope that in this way we will experience some of the sweep, richness, and depth of the gospel. For example, think of the student who when asked to describe *Hamlet* says that it is a tale of a prince driven to avenge the death of his father. While that is true as far as it goes, it hardly does justice to the cathartic depth and power of the play. In the same way, we can say that Jesus was crucified, but that event only begins to be a reality for us as the result of some serious study. So study we must.

In the following and related chapters we will initiate the process of living into the gospel. We will look for places where the path of our story crosses that of Jesus. And it is exactly at that point we find Jesus waiting for us and seeking to bless us. Each chapter ends with questions to spark further thought and discussion.

Finally I invite you to read in whatever way that best serves your needs. Feel free to skip around, or read only the chapters that interest you. I want this book to serve your needs and purposes.

Now we begin our odyssey.

Chapter 1

What in the World!

IMAGINE YOU HAVE PURCHASED tickets to a play and are now sitting in your seat. The theater darkens and the red curtain parts. The scene before you shows various kinds of people walking up and down an imaginary street. One of the characters steps out the scene, walks to the edge of the stage, and addresses the audience.

He is shabbily dressed and nervous, and he begins to weep. "I used to have a great job, but my position was eliminated. I have been desperately looking for work for more than a year, and I can find nothing. I cannot support my family. I am so ashamed. I am a failure every day." He wipes his face and steps back into the street scene.

Next a teenager steps forward. He gives all of his attention to his phone as he taps out text message after text message. He looks up and appears to be surprised that an audience is watching him. "I text all the time, and I get hundreds of texts a day. It's the only fun thing in my life." He pauses and adds, "But I feel lonely most of the time." He continues typing and he turns and rejoins the street scene.

Then a middle-aged woman steps to the front. She is wearing an expensive business suite and her earrings, watch, and necklace gleam with gold. "I am successful, you know. Being a woman has not stopped me for a minute. I am going places. I just hope that people notice my work and my success. I hope I can generate some respect, maybe even a little love." She crisply spins around and goes back to the street scene.

I suspect that most people have little difficulty in identifying with these characters. We know about shame, failure, and the aching desire to be noticed and loved. This imagined drama takes place not only on a stage but in our lives as well.

Most of us seek to find some glimmer of light in the darkness. We try hard to avoid the human tragedies that always seem close at hand, if not inevitable. We long for forgiveness, purpose, hope, love, and a modicum of beauty and justice. This is who we are. This is how we live. This is what we long for.

The question posed by this state of affairs is: what kind of world do we live in. Should we simply learn to accept that our story will be gray, wearisome, and worry-filled? Or could there possibly be a story, an alternative narrative, another reality that would lead us into meaning, hope, and forgiveness?

We begin with the possibility of that alternative narrative. We begin our odyssey.

Enter Jesus. Most of us love Christmas. It is hands-down my favorite holiday. Sunday schools sometimes celebrate is as the birthday of Jesus, but in a deeper sense it asks us to consider the fact of the incarnation. That latinate word proclaims the God who took on flesh, became human, and dwelt among us.

All of the Bible stories we hear in the Christmas season declare the fact of the incarnation, each in its own way. In the gospel of John, for instance, we are told, "And the Word became flesh and lived among us, and we have seen his glory, the glory as of a father's only son, full of grace and truth." (John 1:14) "Word" refers to Jesus, who is the message, the word that God wishes to speak to the world, the story God desires to tell the whole creation. Incidentally, this verse is such a clear, bold, and important declaration of the incarnation that it holds the honor of being the gospel reading for the main service on Christmas day.

The most familiar Christmas account can be found in the second chapter of Luke's gospel. In that narrative the angel assigns important names to the new born child: Savior, Christ, and Lord. The original readers of this gospel would have recognized "Lord" as the traditional title for God in the Old Testament. Born to you this day in the city of David is . . . God incarnate.

Finally, the gospel according to Matthew narrates the story of Jesus birth with an eye to how it fulfills Old Testament prophecy. The evangelist quotes the prophet Isaiah, who wrote, "And they shall name him Emmanuel," (Isa 7:14), and then adds that the name means "God is with us." (Matt 1:23) Again we encounter the incarnation.

When I was growing up I was taught that the two candles on the altar of the church represented the divine and human natures of Christ. This made me wonder, because even at ten or twelve years old I sensed that we were describing a mystery that was beyond my grasp. Years later in seminary I read about the early ecumenical councils of the church and the conflicts involved in trying to describe this mystery of the union of the divine and human by using the categories of Greek philosophy. Both the history of those councils and their deliberations can be at times virtually incomprehensible because the vocabulary they used is unfamiliar to us today. If you want to sample the complexities and sophistication of these early leaders of the church, Google the "Definition of the Union of the Divine and Human Natures in the Person of Christ" from the Council of Chalcedon in 451 AD. These councils and their teaching remain authoritative for the church even today. In their unique way they remind us again that we are dealing with a great mystery.

In the course of my preaching of the over years, then, I have found myself trying to speak of the incarnation in less philosophical ways. For example, I believe we can think of Jesus as the person who was perfectly and completely transparent to God. Or we can speak of Jesus as being totally integrated into God. Or we could say that Jesus is the window into the heart of God. These represent my humble, homiletical attempts to declare the mystery of the incarnation, but I know that they can in no way supplant the historic creeds nor are they adequate to bear the mystery of incarnation. The starting place for me has been to consider that those early disciples who had met and lived with Jesus must have said, "To be in the presence of Jesus is to be in the presence of God." They listened to his teaching and witnessed his mighty acts, and must have concluded, "When he speaks he sounds like God, and when he acts he does those things only God can do." These sorts of personal encounters with Jesus asked people then and now to consider who he is and how we might describe him. Thus arose the doctrine of incarnation, God with us in the flesh.

So far we have been using both metaphors and philosophical language, but now we turn to literary ways of thinking. This approach will open new perspectives for us. With this method the incarnation introduces us to the hero and to the setting of the story. As we move forward we will consider the two other basic elements of a story, plot and dramatic conflict. For example, think of a drawing of a square. At the corners we can write in four terms, hero, setting, plot, and dramatic conflict. That square forms the boundaries of story, and the four categories at the corners define the elements of any story.

To summarize our journey so far, we are seeking a story that serves as the glue of our lives, a story that interprets our existence so that we can live with hope and meaning. I have proposed that the story of Jesus is exactly *that* story, and that it unfolds in four chapters. The first is the incarnation. And using literary categories we are introduced to the main character, the hero, Jesus, as well as to the setting, our world of human thoughts, feelings, imagination, will, and activity.

At this point we need to get a richer and more detailed view of Jesus, and to do that we turn to the gospel according to Luke. The term incarnation introduces us to an intellectual way of meeting Jesus, and I have always found it a helpful code word that I can use to conjure up in my mind a set of stories from the Bible. The term helps me understand, but the stories grasp me and fire my imagination to such an extent that they become the places of living encounters with the divine. Is that not just the sort of story we long for?

Given that, let us look rather carefully at three stories from the New Testament that will usher us into a close encounter with our hero. We begin with what many people mean when they mention "the Christmas story." Regular churchgoers can almost recite it from memory, and it is this narrative that Linus recites in the *Peanuts* Christmas special to explain the meaning of the holiday. I am referring, of course, to chapter two of the gospel according to Luke. Here it is in all its beauty and mystery.

> In those days a decree went out from Emperor Augustus that all the world should be registered. This was the first registration and was taken while Quirinius was governor of Syria. All went to their own towns to be registered. Joseph also went from the town of Nazareth in Galilee to Judea, to the city of David called Bethlehem, because he was descended from the house and family of David. He went to be registered with Mary, to whom he was engaged and who was expecting a child. While they were there, the time came for her to deliver her child. And she gave birth to her firstborn son and wrapped him in bands of cloth, and laid him in a manger, because there was no place for them in the inn. In that region there were shepherds living in the fields, keeping watch over their flock by night. Then an angel of the Lord stood before them, and the glory of the Lord shone around them, and they were terrified. But the angel said to them, "Do not be afraid: for see—I am bringing you good news of great joy for all the people; to you is born this day in the city of David a Savior, who is the Messiah, the Lord. This will be a sign for you: you will find a child wrapped in bands of cloth and lying in a manger" And suddenly there was with the angel a multitude of the heavenly host, praising God and saying,
>
> > Glory to God in the highest heaven,
> > And on earth peace among those whom he favors.
>
> When the angels had left them and gone into heaven, the shepherds said to one another, "Let us go now to Bethlehem and see this thing that has taken place, which the Lord has made known to us." So they went with hast and found Mary and Joseph and the child lying in the manger. When they saw this, they made known what had been told them about this child; and all who heard it were amazed at what the shepherds told them. But Mary

treasured all these words and pondered them in her heart. The shepherds returned, glorifying and praising God for all they had heart and seen, as it had been told them. (Luke 2:1–20)

To step back a bit the first chapter of Luke's gospel reminds me of a scene from medieval stained glass. Beautifully written, they have a pleasing archaic quality. They are colorful and moving narratives, which begin what the evangelist calls on "orderly account of the events that have been fulfilled among us." (Luke 1:1) We read about the announcements of the births of both Jesus and John the Baptist, the visit of the two pregnant mothers with each other, and the astonishing events surrounding the birth of John the Baptist. Now the stage is set for the appearance of Jesus.

The account begins with a remarkable set of statements that situate the birth of Jesus firmly in time and space. So we are not to understand this as an entertaining tale or another myth about the lives of the gods. This is history in a strict sense. The time is during the reign of Caesar Augustus (63 BC–14 AD), the first Roman emperor, the ruler who brought peace to the empire, and who even encouraged the worship of his "genius," his divine spirit, at altars around the empire. Also mentioned is Quirinius, the appointed governor of the imperial province of Syria. Jesus, then, born in a period when Rome had become an empire, when the power of the state was growing, and when the emperor himself was seen as the deity who enjoyed the titles of "savior" and "lord."

Nazareth, at that time, was a village in the northern part of the Holy Land, and Bethlehem, a few miles south of Jerusalem, serve as the setting for our story. Nazareth was a place of little account in those days, but Bethlehem was famed as the birth place of David, the great King who had led God's people into an unsurpassed gold age about a millennium before Jesus' birth. Furthermore, the ancient prophets foretold Bethlehem as the birthplace of the Messiah, the "anointed one," whom people hoped would appear as a new David and lead them into a second gold age. In short, the town was fraught with history and divine possibility, even at a time when the titles savior, lord, and messiah were buzzing in the conversation of the people.

Extra-biblical sources have no record of Augustus authorizing a census, but they do indicate that Quirinius carried out a tally of his people. The purpose of such a census was to collect data for the purposes of taxation, but is also served to remind the people that they were under the mighty thumb of Rome. Moreover, it was an irritant to Jewish people, who held a long-standing animosity toward any sort of census; they believed that counting the people of God was the business of God alone.

So we find Joseph and Mary making their way to Bethlehem, the ancestral home of Joseph. In a later chapter of this gospel, the evangelists traces Jesus' genealogy through Joseph all the way back to David himself (Luke 3:23–38). The climax of the episode is told in the simplest language possible. While in Bethlehem Jesus, the son of David, was born in the back room of an inn or home, because there were no vacancies in the rooms of the inns.

My younger daughter was born under unusual, even awkward, circumstances. My wife and I had made it as far as the doctor's office, but things were happening too quickly to proceed to the hospital. The doctor was busy with another patient, and my wife, lying in an examining room, was beginning to panic, certain that a birth was imminent. After what seemed like an eternity the doctor appeared carrying a cup of coffee in one hand and a cigarette in the other. "So, what's going on in here?" he asked. Minutes later Rachel arrived. Even as an adult she loves to hear the who, what, when, and where of her birth. It has a grounding effect on her. It makes the real more real. The story of Jesus' nativity has the same effect on us in that it helps us grasp the "What's going on in here." It grounds Jesus for us.

Luke so far has told us about the time and place, the milieu, of Jesus' birth, and he has done so in a manner that firmly situates the divine in the human context. But more remains to be said. To the sound of fluttering angel wings the evangelists investigates the further significance of the birth of this humble child.

It's a scene reiterated in many carols and holiday cards. Some shepherds were tending their sheep at night, and are stunned by the appearance of an angel, who has entered the human sphere to proclaim news that interprets Jesus' birth. The message can be summarized this way:

Do not be afraid.

I bring good news.

It was cause great joy for all people.

Born in David's city is the savior, who is messiah and lord.

Note especially the three titles given to Jesus. The lineage of Joseph and his birth in Bethlehem have already hinted that he is the long-expected successor to David, although we will see that the nature of his kingdom and power differs from that of his distinguished ancestor.

He is also named savior and lord. For the citizens of Rome this would be shocking, even subversive, news. They honored the emperor Augustus with those title, but here they are bestowed on a baby. Moreover, Jewish people would have reserved those two honorifics for God alone. Not only has the angel come from heaven to earth, but, God, too has made that journey to be the Incarnate One, the Savior, Messiah, and Lord.

As if this were not enough a chorus of angels appears and sings a song of praise, "Glory to God in the highest heaven, and on earth peace among those who he favors." (Luke 2:14) This child will be a peace bearer, giving his followers all they need to worship and serve God with joy.

We can easily identify Luke's world of politics, power, and potentates. Things haven't changed much. But it astonishes us that God has become incarnate among the poor, among the animals. This baffles the mind, but moves the heart. And here's why. This story says that God is at work in the world and among human beings. God has rolled up divine sleeves and begun the work of giving life and peace. It says that God has exercised divine freedom to move into our world of time and space. God has cared enough to lay down divine glory. It says God have come among us embodied in Jesus.

I was at a visiting museum some time back. A women was demonstrating the eighteenth century way of making cloth. She was laboring over a loom, with fierce concentration arranging horizontal and vertical threads. Next came a forceful jerk on the loom, adding another line to the cloth. From where I was looking she was putting together a beautiful design. From a few yards away the cloth appeared seamless and smooth, but at close range I could see the careful, delicate weave. The divine and the human with all their detail were seamlessly and smoothly woven together by God. The incarnation. God with us.

Next, we consider the story of the incarnation from another angle. Let me tell still another story about my two daughters when both were in high school. Late one afternoon I received an excited phone call. They had been out in our car doing some chores, and they had been involved in an accident. A tractor trailer had side-swiped them. No one was hurt, but they were, nevertheless worried about the damage to the car. There were seven witnesses to the accident: the truck driver, four pedestrians, and my daughters. The police arrived and interviewed these people. Would you believe that every one of them had a different account, seven witnesses with seven stories?

We should not be surprised or shocked, then, that we have several accounts of the incarnation. For instance, Luke's narrative emphasizes the role of the Virgin Mary, but Matthew takes his cues from Joseph. Not only that, both emphasized different aspects of incarnation. We look now to this second account by Matthew in order to probe more deeply into the incarnational mystery.

> Now the birth of Jesus the Messiah took place in this way.
> Then his mother Mary had been engaged to Joseph, but
> before they had lived together, she was found to be with
> child from the Holy Spirit. Her husband Joseph, being
> a righteous man and unwilling to expose her to public
> disgrace, planned to dismiss her quietly. But just when he
> had resolved to do this, and angel of the Lord appeared to

him in a dream and said, "Joseph, son of David, do not be afraid to take Mary as your wife, for the child conceived in her is from the Holy Spirit. She will bear a son, and you are to name him Jesus, for he will save his people from their sins." All this took place to fulfill what had been spoken by the Lord through the prophet:

> "Look, the virgin shall conceive and bear a son,
> and they shall name him Emmanuel,"

which means "God is with us." When Joseph awoke from sleep, he did has the angel of the Lord had commanded him; he took her as his wife, but had no marital relations with her until she had borne a son, and he named him Jesus. (Matt 1:18–25)

We immediately note that Joseph has a big problem on his hands, namely, his betrothed is pregnant and he is not the father. And he lived in a society that had a great deal to say about this situation.

The issues go this way. Jewish culture at that time saw betrothal and marriage as serious matters, so serious, in fact, that there existed many legal and societal boundaries around them. When a woman was betrothed—and that could happen as early as early as twelve years old—the perspective groom would present to her father a marriage contract and pay a bride-price. They were now officially betrothed, but lived apart, the woman remaining in the home of and under the protection of her father. After a year or more the wedding itself took place. The heart of the ceremony was the procession of the bride from her father's house to the house of the groom. You sense, I hope, the legal and cultural factors: a contract made, money exchanged, public attestation. I cannot help but think that in village life all of this was given careful scrutiny by everyone.

The problem was Mary's unexplained pregnancy. My guess is that even if she had told people that she was pregnant by the presence and power of God no one would have believed her. And who can blame them? The ancient law of Israel prescribed the death penalty for a woman in Mary's situation; this was understood as a matter of purging sin from the community as well as restoring honor to her father. In fairness we need to add that there is no historical record that this harsh punishment ever being carried out.

The evangelist then shares with us Joseph's decision about how he will handle this hot-potato issue. He resolves to divorce Mary. At that time divorce was a simple affair. Joseph would have written a letter telling Mary of his intention and that would be witnessed by two other men. Upon delivery of the letter the divorce was effected, and Mary would return to her father's home.

Joseph chose a rather private and delicate way to treat Mary, sparing her from as much shame and public attention as possible. We are told that he made this choice because he was righteous man, that is, a person who always tried to do what was right according to God's will.

So far we have two people with one big problem. But now God gets involved. In scripture one of the favored ways that God communicates with people is in and through dreams. So, God's angel appears to Joseph in his dreams.

The first angelic word to Joseph is that he should not be afraid. Then follow two more instructions. First, take Mary as your wife, because her pregnancy is the result of the Holy Spirit, and, second, the son should be named Jesus.

The name is no small matter, in as much as in the Bible a person's name could reveal something important about his or her character. Jesus' name means "God is our help," or "God saves." So this name later will function as a job description of his public ministry. It's not surprise, then, that the church sets aside a day in the liturgical calendar to call attention to his name; it is called The Holy Name of Our Lord Jesus Christ, always celebrated on January 1. Sometimes names do matter.

The climax of Matthew's narrative arrives when it is majestically announced "that all this took place to fulfill what had been spoken by the Lord through the prophet Isaiah. (Mt 1:22) The evangelists wants us to understand that the incarnation was not a last-minute, put-up affair, but rather had always been in the mind of God, and that God had been at work through the centuries and through Israel to prepare for the appearing of Jesus.

Matthew then quotes the eighth century BC prophet Isaiah. In its original setting the prophet is told by God to seek out Ahaz, the king of Judah, and give him a divine message. Judah is under threat of attack from two of its neighbors, and Ahaz is considering aligning his kingdom with the superpower Assyria to fend off his enemies. God's message is that Ahaz should depend on God and not on alliances with other nations. To shore up the message, Isaiah offers a sign to the king. In paraphrase, he says, "See that young women there? She will have a child named Emmanuel, and before he can tell the difference between good and evil, God will have acted in a decisive way." So the little boy Emmanuel, which means "God with us," will become a walking sign of the power and intervention of God. You can read the full account in Isaiah chapter 7.

That's the sense of the prophecy in its original 735 BC setting. But the evangelist sees a further dimension to Isaiah's message in the person of Jesus. That ancient prophetic word is about to take on new life and will fulfill the prophecy in an unforeseen way. Jesus will be the new Emmanuel, a walking sign, this time of God's saving intervention for the sake of all humanity. Even more, he will *be* God's saving presence.

To me it's clear that the evangelist Matthew is deeply moved by the continuing vitality of the ancient words of the Old Testament, and, therefore, he uses fulfillment language more than fifteen times in his gospel. For him God's plans for peace and salvation are about to reach their fruition in the incarnation. And it is not a matter of God standing out the world pulling strings, but rather that God jumps into the deep end of the pool by becoming incarnate, just according to prophecy.

We have still one more version of the incarnation to explore. I experienced college as both a time of intense intellectual excitement and of intense intellectual challenge. I had lazed my way through high school, but found myself in a very selective school where the faculty held students to high standards. In looking back on that time I remember especially two classes.

As a freshman I took a class entitle "Western Civilization." Today that course would be considered too Eurocentric and parochial, but it did me a world of good to ponder the history of the culture in which I live and which I love. Our instructor had previously taught in a Jesuit school in Europe and now unleashed his vast store of knowledge on a group of humble freshman largely from the Midwest. The first exam left me stunned. I had been accustomed to history tests that wanted lists of dates and summaries of events. But his exam assumed that we had the raw data in mind, and thus he posed more difficult "compare and contrast" and "write an essay about the significance of" questions. I had to learn a new intellectual skill, being able to see the big picture.

As a sophomore I enrolled in a basic biology class in order to fulfill an institutional requirement for a degree. The demands of the class were huge: five days a week of 8 AM lectures, several hours per week in small group recitation sessions, and lab work that often stretched to six or eight hours a week. And that does not take into account the reading and study involved. The truth is that I became resentful of the demands of a class in which I had only a mild interest. I found the lab sessions especially irritating. When I went I had no idea how long I would be there, and we were always looking at tiny life forms through a microscope, and then we were to draw what we saw in detail. My irritation was aggravated by my astigmatic eyes, which do not work well with microscopes. In that class, I had to persist in learning the small details, to look at tiny things, and to remember it all. Attention to the details, this, too, was a new intellectual discipline.

Our look at the incarnational stories from Luke and Matthew has been akin to my work in biology class. We have studied the details of the accounts, taken into consideration the contexts, and have tried to appreciate the richness of these narratives.

Now we move to the other approach, the approach demanded by my history instructor. We must look at the big picture and try to grasp the great theme of incarnation in a cosmic context. We know the details. Now we step back and consider a broad, even universal, view. And this is exactly what the soaring prologue to the gospel of John lays before us.

In the beginning was the Word, and the Word was with God, and the Word was God. He was in the beginning with God. All things came into being through him, and without him, not one thing came into being. What has come into being in him was life, and the life was the light of all people. The light shine in the darkness, and the darkness did not over come it . . . The true light, which enlightens everyone, was coming into the world. He was in the world, and the world came into being through him; yet the world did not know him. He came to what was his own, and his own people did not accept him. But to all who received him, who believed in his name, he gave power to become the children of God, who were born, not of blood or of the will of the flesh or of the will of man, but of God. And the Word became flesh and lived among us, and we have seen his glory, the glory as of a father's only son, full of grace and truth . . . From his fullness we have all receive, grace upon grace. The law indeed was given through Moses; grace and truth came through Jesus Christ. No one has ever seen God. It is God's only Son, who is close to the Father's heart, who has made him known. (John 1:1–5, 9–14, 16–18)

The traditional symbol for John's gospel is an eagle. I do not know the official story about how this came to be, but I have my own theory. These introductory verses give an eagle's eye view of Jesus. This and many other passages further along in this gospel give us the big picture. Further, I think of eagles flying from the heavens with breathtaking rapidity. I live in Montana, where both bald and golden eagles thrive; they are simply beautifully majestic creatures. So, too, John's gospel astounds us with its majesty and beauty. These qualities are on full display in the prologue.

Let's soar with the eagle. First, note that John is not concerned with the details. We have no mention of Bethlehem, the manger, or angels. Instead we find something like a theological poem about the pre-existence of Christ and about his manifestation among us.

The evangelists nobly proclaims the theme of the eternal, pre-existent Christ, who is both the means through which God created all things and who is the goal of all things. So John can justifiably speak of him as divine light and life.

Verses fourteen and fifteen stand as the key passage, the summary of the prologue. "And the Word became flesh and lived among us, and we have seen his glory, the glory of a father's only son, full of grace and truth." The evangelists invites us to view the rest of the gospel through the lens of these verses, which proclaim Jesus as the Word made flesh.

We cannot side-step careful attention to the word "Word." This gospel along with the rest of the New Testament is written in Greek, and in that language 'Word' is *Logos*. We quickly recognize that terms as part of such English words of logic and biology. There is a book-worth of things one can say about this term, but let me offer a short summary.

First, it is "word" in the sense that what we speak communicates who we are. Hurtful comments suggest a callous and angry individual, for example. Word are the agents of contact between human beings in a way that is more specific and nuanced than any other mode of communication. I can, for instance, see a certain sort of expression on my wife's face that hints at her love for me, but I can move to a high level of certainty when she speaks the words "I love you." That is one sense of *Logos*, an important idea expressed.

A second nuance of the term expands on the first. This usage implies a public announcement of something significant. On our national day of July 4 we enjoy hearing again the Declaration, the *Logos*, of Independence. It inspires us today to maintain freedom and liberty, but in 1776 it was a carefully wrought and public statement of what the people in the American colonies wanted to say to the British monarch. And its inflammatory and subversive content insured the interest of George III. So we have *Logos* as a public announcement of important matters.

A third sense of *Logos* shifts the meaning in a bit of a new direction. The emphasis now is suggested by our word "logic." The evangelist seeks to point us to the manner in which a mind works, to the process of thinking. In this third nuance, then, the evangelist is proclaiming Jesus as the logic of God's mind. If you want to know how and what God is thinking, look to Jesus. If you desire to know the logic of God, consider the Word made flesh, the Incarnate One.

John's understanding of Jesus as the Word allows us to cover the ground of Luke and Matthew at a deeper level. Luke speaks of the virginal conception of Jesus to point us to the insight that Jesus is divine, sent from God, even as he is at the same time human by virtue of Mary being his mother. So it was early councils of the church gave Mary the title Theotokos, the God bearer or the Mother of God, a term that tells us more about Jesus than his mother. Moreover, in the message of the angel Luke anticipates the future public ministry of Jesus as Savior, Christ, and Lord.

Matthew, too, wants us to reflect on the mystery of the perfect mix of full divinity and full humanity in Jesus. The one whose very name means savior is also and exactly the Emmanuel, the prophetic fulfillment of the declaration that God is with us.

That brings us back to John. In the term *Logos* all of these themes are pulled together in a single title.

So where have we been so far in our quest for a story that brings life and peace? The first chapter of our four-part narrative can be summed up in a single word, incarnation, the Word made flesh. But what depth is contained therein! It is as if we open a simple door into a room filled with gold, silver, and jewels. Please note that it takes narrative, story, to lay before us these riches, and we have tried to dig deeply into the wonders contained in this story.

Along the way I have used the word mystery again and again. I have done so with some reluctance, because I think in everyday language it denotes something we cannot understand or explain. But when we approach scripture we should think of it in another sense. In the Bible a mystery is not so much something beyond our understanding, although there may be an element of that, but rather as a person or event so full of meaning that we cannot take it all in. A mystery invites exploration and analysis, even though we should not expect to get to the bottom of it. Incarnation fits fully into this second definition.

You may remember from algebra class those wonderful drawings called Venn diagrams. They consist simply of sets of overlapping circles, each representing a distinct quantity or idea. Please think about the following Venn diagram as a way of summarizing our study. In your mind draw three circles that overlap. One represents our story, both the shape and the details of our lives, and the second represents the story of the world in which we live, our current context. The third circle stands for God's story as told in the Bible. In your mind's eye you can see an area at the center formed by the overlapping of the three circles. This can be for us the place of life, peace, and meaning. We already know almost without thinking about our stories and the story of our world. But what happens when we intersect those with the story of God revealed, made incarnate in Jesus, the Savior, the Christ, the Word, and the Emmanuel? At that place we can live the mystery of God being with us with depth and richness. And best of all we can begin the adventure of living life to the full.

These wonderful stories from Matthew, Luke, and John announce the breathtaking news that God has been among us in the deepest and most personal sense. God was a specific person, living in a specific time and place. God was a person who ate, slept, and experienced all that human beings know, think, and feel.

The divine became human. This dignifies our minds, bodies, imagination, thoughts, and wills. St. Paul uses a striking image which captures this. In 1 Corinthians he states that our bodies are the temple of the Holy Spirit. (1 Cor 6:19) This image only makes sense in light of the incarnation understood in its deepest sense.

The incarnation is a sign of how much we are valued by God Again, Paul in Philippians goes to the heart of the matter when he quotes what appears to be an early Christian hymn: "Christ Jesus, who, though he was in the form of God, did not regard equality with God as something to be exploited, but emptied himself, taking the form of a slave, being born in human likeness." (Phil 2:5–7) In poetic language we can say the Jesus gave it all up in order to be with us. That is how much we are valued!

To conclude, we note three questions for which the incarnation supplies answers. First, where is God? God is in our world, in our lives, among us. The incarnation is the paradigm and basis for this. What is God like? God is active in love to bless us with joy and peace. How do we know this? We look to Jesus and his incarnation.

So that is the first stage of our journey with Jesus. We enter into the mystery of incarnation.

Some questions to chew on:

First, define incarnation in your own words. Keep it concise.

Second, if you were designing a Christmas card, what would be the picture on the front and what would be the greeting inside?

Third, if you and your church were to develop a ministry that expressed the meaning of incarnation, what might that be?

Fourth, what do you imagine Jesus looked like? What might it have been like to meet him?

Chapter 2

Inhabiting the Incarnation

IN THE PREVIOUS CHAPTER we looked at the narratives of the birth of Jesus as found in Matthew, Luke, and John. We used the theological term "incarnation" as a code word to refer to the stories of Jesus' nativity. We noted that they are rich indeed with detail and depth. They all witness to the astonishing gospel message that God has come among us, shared in the fullness of our humanity, and partook completely in life, limited as it is by time and space. And we used the word "mystery" as a description of this event, something so full of meaning that we cannot hope to comprehend or explain it fully. All of this deals with a basic life question: how shall we shape the journey of our lives. What attitudes, ideas, and images will guide us in our choices, decision, and the assumption we make?

What if we were to inhabit fully this incarnational reality? We are human beings who dwell in a certain time and place, and we are proscribed by a variety of factors. All of this describes Jesus, too. He has fully lived our reality. What might it look like if we decided to inhabit his reality? I used to have a friend one of whose favorite by-lines was, "We'll just have to live into that." How might we be transformed if we lived into the incarnation? The task of this chapter is to explore that possibility.

First, incarnational people live with a vibrant sense of the presence of God. If the incarnation demonstrates anything it is that God chooses to be with us, fully involved in our lives, in the church, and in the world. The Christian religion in no way teaches a distant, detached deity, who is beyond any concern about the world or its inhabitants. The incarnation says "no" to any teaching of a clock-work divinity, who created the universe and then stepped aside to let it tick away.

Moreover, when God is present peace and blessings follow. Remember the angels in Luke's gospel proclaim the advent of a new age of peace. Matthew proclaims a prophecy fulfilled in the coming of a new sort of ruler, who would usher in the rule of God. And John describes Jesus as the bringer of grace and truth. From my own point of view, Christians would be more effective agents of God if we were to cast aside our sad ambiguity about the good news of the incarnation. No room exists for sentiments such as God is displeased with us, God has to be appeased, or God metes out punishment. Incarnation is clear: God chooses to be present granting rich blessings from a bottomless supply of grace.

Given that, why are we so plagued with fear and worry? My personal analysis is that these two factors of fear and worry are the most prominent and characteristic feelings of our culture. We are experts at both. We are constantly bombarded with the message that we are unimportant and inadequate people, and that Christ's church is a feckless organization. Dare I say that our whole system of materialistic capitalism is fueled by that assumption that unimportant and inadequate people always want something, almost anything, to cure their fear and worry? If I only had that sporty Cadillac sedan perhaps people would think I am exciting and desirable. Or that new pair of shoes would make me more glamorous. On and on it goes. All the time. Everywhere. And it reaches its climax in the secular celebration of Christmas: all will be well if we decorate festively enough, if we purchase just the right gifts, if we serve the perfect Christmas dinner. Ironic, isn't it?

We need to work on developing a manger mentality. Even in bad circumstances—and clearly delivering a baby in someone else's barn and then using a feeding trough as a bed is less than a good situation—God can be present with gifts of grace, truth, and peace. And the truth is that most of us most of time feel as if we are out back in a shabby barn with little to offer. And yet, that exactly describes where Jesus is born, both in the past in Bethlehem and today among us.

John's gospel, moreover, states that the incarnation brings "grace upon grace." That word grace refers to the fact that we enjoy the unmerited favor of God simply because God chooses to be graceful. The little phrase "grace upon grace" suggests abundance, lavishness, and plenitude. God's blessings don't trickle, but rather burst upon us. God is not the miserly old man who slips a nickel into the hand of a child and says, "There's a nice gift for you." God has a Fort Knox supply of blessings. It is always grace upon grace.

I live in Helena, the capital city of Montana, and it certainly qualifies as one of the great small cities in the country. The story of its birth goes this way. In the 1860's four brave souls were prospecting for gold in the high desert wilderness of the Rockies. They had traveled far and had found nothing. They were about to give up and return home to Georgia, but decided to try one small trickle of a stream flowing down the side of a mountain. They had decided that this would be their last chance to discover gold. To their joy and surprise they found gold, and lots of it. Over the next decades gold worth hundreds of millions of dollars was found, and Helena became one of the richest cities in the country. That can, I think, serve as a parable. A little gold washed out of the mud of an unimposing stream results in the birth of a wonderful city. God works in similar ways. When we are at the end of our rope, God is able and willing to pour out abundantly golden blessings.

The manger mentality functions on the basis of a confidence in God's willingness to bless. Can we lay aside assumptions about scarcity, that we do not have enough money, time, talent, or whatever in order to step up into the reality of the incarnation? I believe that we as persons and as church can live with a vibrant confidence in God's abundance. The incarnation stands as the proof of God's desire to be with us giving graceful blessing.

Fresh out of seminary I arrived at my first church, a small mission congregation. I knew that they had been receiving financial support from the national church for many years and that they carried a large mortgage on their building. But imagine my shock when one of the stalwart members informed me, "Before you came we had to decide if we wanted to close or to call you."

I was stunned. This was a set of circumstances that drove me to my knees in fear and worry. What if I failed? Would that end my "career" in the church? Could I live with being a big-time loser? But God was about to teach me a life lesson. The constant word that came to me in prayer and in study of scripture was that I was to soldier on and do my best, and that that would suffice. As the months unfolded blessings began to break out. The vestry decided that they no longer needed mission support. They decided that a good Sunday school program was within our abilities. On and on it went. Through it all I began to learn manger mentality. I learned that when God is present, blessings will follow.

Second, we would learn to accept surprises. One of the illusions that we persist in holding is that if we work, think, and plan hard enough we will be able to control the future. And we do that because we are enamored of the idea that our abilities allow us to determine our future.

When I was in college I enrolled in a course entitle "Future Studies." Popular at the time was Alvin Toffler's *Future Shock*, which took a stab at predicting changes coming in the future. In our class we developed a list of problems facing our society, did some research, and discussed our thinking about the shape of things to come. As I look back over the decades at what we thought was going to be the issues and what we proposed as solution, I can say that we got it wrong on almost every count. It was a semester spent on the assumption that we could get an accurate view of the future and could plan for it. Our goal was to eliminate surprise.

If the incarnation is a reality, then we need to give up our little exercises in future studies and begin to appropriate the fact that God is actually at work among us in surprising ways. To put another way, we can neither foresee nor control God's future. But that is OK, because God's future is blessing. For instance, many of Jesus' contemporaries were looking for a messiah who would be a descendent of David and, like David, be a military and political leader who would initiate a new golden age for Israel. Jesus was the messiah, but what he embodied was the Reign of God as the realm of peace and grace. That was such a surprise that some were simply not able to comprehend Jesus.

All the congregations I served, for example, came as a surprise to me. And I never imagined that I would be a bishop. Most of the people to whom I took a dislike have turned out to be a blessing to me. I have certainly been bowled over by what God can accomplish through God's people.

It was all surprise. So as persons and as church we need to be flexible about what we hope and plan for. We need to give up being stunned when we learn that we are not the masters of our souls and the captains of our fate. Like children opening Christmas gifts, we can rightly think, "And what wonderful thing is in here for me?" In the final analysis nothing could be more of a surprise than the reality of the incarnation.

When I was working on a doctoral dissertation I had to explain what I had hoped to learn in the process of my work and also what unexpected learning had occurred. The surprise was not only how many unexpected developments there were, but also that they were the most important of my learnings. Similarly God loves to astonish us with unplanned graces. We can practice being flexible about the surprises God has in store for us, exactly because God will be with us in the surprises granting blessing upon blessing.

In one of the churches of which I was rector we were thinking about remodeling the chancel area. A long-time member told me what I thought of that possibility. "I am opposed," he said, "to all change whatsoever." What he may have been saying was, "Please do not ask me to be flexible enough to accommodate God's presence and activity." He had missed the adventure, the surprise, and the blessing.

Three, if the incarnation is a reality we will learn to value ourselves. I know that in declaring that I am walking down a potentially dangerous path. Today we are committed to the ideas of "self-esteem" and "to feeling good about ourselves." Those factors are, of course, rooted in accomplishment. So, a child does well on an exam, and the teacher puts a gold star at the top of the page. Or a woman works hard at her job and thereby earns a promotion.

I hope, however, that you can sense a problem. This view says that we have a right to feel good about ourselves, and that we can do what it takes to accomplish that. But as the years pass I have had to admit that my life, at least, is a murky affair. I have accomplished some good things, but with them came some costs and pain, often involving other people. Accomplishments are gray affairs, neither entirely good or bad. At best, I carry a C average in my life journey.

Moreover, relishing our victories and attainments can cause us to develop moral myopia. We effortlessly begin to think that we alone have done some worthy thing, forgetting that we never live solitary lives. I can make a tasty cake, and feel good about that. But who made the flour and butter, who developed and printed the recipe, and who provided the electricity for the stove?

Accomplishments never occur in isolation.

But there exists another and a better way to appraise ourselves. The incarnation cuts through the murkiness, and declares that Almighty God values us. We are the apple of God's eye. As John's gospel succinctly puts it, God so loved the world that he sent his only son. (John 3:16) We are, then, loved into a sense of our own dignity and worth. Ascetical theology teaches a concept called divinization, that God became human so that humanity might become divine. Therein lies our value and our worth. The gold stars and promotions come from God.

I once served on the board of directors of an agency that provided residential care for teenage boys, most of whom had been referred there by a juvenile court. One of the most valuable experiences was provided by two retired men, who offered a class in woodworking. At the end of the class most of the boys had made a beautiful end table or storage chest. The director of the agency said, "This is the first time these boys have accomplished anything good." And it transformed those teens. But it happened because those young men were guided and loved into transformation. God works that way with us all.

Four, we would more highly value the material world. I had a professor who was fond of saying that all of western philosophy was simply a footnote to Plato. It would be hard to overestimate his importance to the way we think, even today. One of Plato's basic teachings declared that what was most important and most real were what he termed the ideals. These belonged only in the realm of thought and were essentially the perfect prototypes of everything in the material world. That is, everything we see and know is an imperfect replica of the heavenly ideals. It followed that what was material, including the environment and the human body, were imperfect and of lesser worth. Many of us have been living Plato more than the incarnation.

An instance of the problem is our environmental crisis. The earth, the seas, and water have not been especially high on our list important matters. Could it be that we value the ideas of profit and progress more? Jesus was not a Platonist, and neither should we be.

The situation gets even more complicated. Our religious expectation tend toward what some call "the spiritual." This often means that we search for an internal religious experience that is exciting and inspiring, the proverbial mountain top experience. These feelings and the search for them become the substance of the religion for some. The consequence is that they become intensely focused on their own inner lives. Is this not a variation of a theme by Plato? This thinking collides with the reality of Jesus, born in a manger. To look at him is to view God in the flesh. Our faith centers itself in him, not on inner emotional excitations, not matter how pleasant. Jesus *is* the mountain top experience, and religious emotions are secondary to him.

I would find it enormously refreshing if the church were both to take more leadership in the care of the earth and to find ways to focus more on Jesus, son of Mary. In doing that we would be taking hold of our own full humanity and offering it to God. That would be inspiring!

As I write snow has fallen in Montana, lots of it. This morning I was shoveling the driveway, and a little gift wandered into the yard. I asked for her name. "Michaela, and I'm her granddaughter," she said while pointing to our neighbor. At that moment I became a bit edgy, because I wanted to be friendly but was not sure what to do. So, I pointed to my dog, and said, "That's Lizzie." Michaela asked, "Does she do tricks?" I replied, "If you bend down and say, 'kiss-kiss' she will give you a kiss." She bent down, said the magic word, and received the promised dog kiss. She then waved and went into the house. What more could you want than a kiss, especially a kiss from the best dog in the world. It was that real, material act of a kiss that made my morning and probably Michaela's, too.

In the incarnation God kissed the world. Jesus' nativity is God's hug of humanity. Let's attend to that fact.

Next, the incarnation makes us people of gratitude and obedience. One of the large greeting card companies used to have as its motto, "When you care enough to send the very best."

That describes what God has done for us in the incarnation. God has send the best, God's own self, to become one of us.

So, how do we respond? If we receive a greeting card that says exactly the right thing at the right time, we are likely to say, "I'll have to thank her for that." Gratitude and thanksgiving constitute the proper responses to a message that speaks directly to us and our situation.

Those of us who have raised children, however, know that neither of these virtues come naturally to human beings. They have to be inculcated. I often hear a particular little litany between parents and children after a gift or a kind word has been given. Parent: what do you say? Child: thank you. Could we not say that gratitude is simply good manners toward God?

If we take a long view, we see that everything is gift. Everything is grace. From that flows a life of gratitude and thanksgiving. But we do have to work at developing it.

Years ago I developed the habit of beginning my daily private prayer by thanking God for gifts and graces. Sometimes large and important matter come to mind: my wife, my work, even the incarnation. But sometimes it is small things: the comfortable chair I am sitting in or a good breakfast. This devotional practice has been transformative for me. Daily I see gift upon gift being heaped on me.

When we have reached that place of gratitude we find that it morphs into obedience. I am an Episcopalian, and as you would expect I find great value in The Book of Common Prayer. It includes what are staples of life for me, Morning and Evening Prayer. Both end with the General Thanksgiving, which says, "Give us such an awareness of your mercies, that with truly thankful hearts we may show forth your praise, not only with our lips, but in our lives, by giving up our selves to your service, and by walking before you in holiness and righteousness all our days." (p 101) Note the movement from thanksgiving to gratitude to obedience. Part of the insight and wisdom of this prayer is that obedience takes the form of service and holiness. This is not a matter of moralism or trying to follow the rules. It is, rather, seeking to live close to Jesus and to serve others just as he did. That is obedience. From a life filled with gratitude we are shaped by the Risen Christ into people who can become a source of gratitude for others.

I recently made a hospital call on a friend who was in the intensive care unit of the hospital, and things frankly did not look hopeful for her. Despite that again and again she declared, "I am so blessed by God." Then she enumerated her blessings. I came away abashed by how much worry and complaining I indulge in, and I was also inspired by her gratitude to practice more of the same in my life.

Finally, people of the incarnation value the Holy Eucharist. Years ago I read a statement that has stuck with me: if the incarnation is possible, then Christ's real presence in the Eucharist is also possible. In this astonishing sacrament incarnation, thanksgiving, obedience, gift, and all the other factors we have been exploring come together in what surely constitutes the high point in the life of Christians.

I once leafed through a children's illustrated guide to the Eucharist. One of the pages pictured an altar of a church, and present above the altar the artist had drawn the image of the Lord himself. That simple picture has been the source of comfort and meditation for me as I prepare to receive Christ in the bread and wine of the sacrament. The incarnation one is as present in the Eucharist as he was in the manger in Bethlehem.

As a parish priest I had the privilege of training children to receive their first communion.

The instruction contained a number of elements, including the Eucharist as a family meal at which Jesus is present, how to use the Prayer Book, and how to kneel at the altar rail. I always asked them as they were receiving the bread to put one hand on top of the other. "Make your hands a little manger to hold Christ," I said. To live into the incarnation is to develop a life both centered in the Eucharist, so that we ourselves become a manger in which he dwells.

Some years back I was privileged to be part of a month-long study course in the Holy Land. On the first Sunday there we made our way through the streets of the Old City of Jerusalem to a church of the Orthodox tradition. I was aware of some aspects of Orthodoxy's doctrine and piety, but I was not prepared for what I encountered that day. As I stepped in to the church a wave of color swept over me; the ceiling, walls, and pillars of the building were covered with icon-like images. My eyes were first captured by a huge image of Christ, which seemed to float above the altar. He was pictured as the Risen Christ, sitting on a throne, the Pantocrator, the judge of all things. Nearby was the Blessed Virgin Mary, cloaked in an azure robe. In dazzling array I saw apostles, evangelists, saints, martyrs, confessors, and scores of angels. I was caught up in this vision of the beauty of holiness. As the liturgy began there were clouds of incense and full-throated singing. That bright morning I had stepped into a new reality, a vision of the world transformed by the fact of the incarnation.

We, in fact, inhabit that reality all the time, a world of wonder and mystery. Oh, that we had eyes to see!

Some questions to help you inhabit the incarnation:

First, as you think about the familiar Christmas story from Luke's gospel, what phrase or element most holds your attention? Why? What might God be saying to you through this story?

Second, what change do I need to make better to live into the incarnation? What changes does my church need to make to be more incarnational?

Third, as you think about your journey through life, what are three occasion when you have been most aware that God was active in your life? As you observe the life of your congregation where do you think people are most likely to be encountered by Christ?

Fourth, in what ways might the fact of the incarnation help you conquer fear and worry?

Chapter 3

The Beloved

JESUS HIMSELF LEADS US into the second phase of his journey. In the previous chapter we explored the narratives that we sum up with the word "incarnation". We worked on one of the foundational questions which all people and institutions raise: in what sort of world will we make our sojourn through life. The incarnation declares that the world is the setting for incarnation, that God is with us in the odyssey of life. Even more the incarnation proclaims not just divine presence, but that God has taken on the materiality of our lives and world. God is not just with us, but also among us and in us. The spirituality of this we have called inhabiting the incarnation.

Jesus is now ready to inaugurate the second phase of his journey. We know from the gospel account that the substance of his message was the kingdom, the rule, of God. That phrase refers to the place, to the sphere of existence, where God's will is done. Remember Jesus' prayer: your kingdom come, your will be done. Jesus will go through the towns and villages of Galilee, and later Judea, healing the sick, exorcising demons, feeding the hungry, accepting sinners, revivifying the dead, and granting the forgiveness of sins. That, he seems to declare, is what it looks like when God rules. Moreover, Jesus's teaching explains the sovereignty of God in order to challenge people to open their eyes and see the work of God as a present and active reality. It soon becomes clear in the gospels that Jesus constitutes the rule of God in his own person; he *is* the kingdom.

But first Jesus deals with one of the basic issues of human existence: identity. As he was about to step onto the public stage of history he needed to clarify who he was at the most basic level of life. What titles, what adjectives, what declarations might state the foundational selfhood of Jesus.

When I was in college and seminary in the sixties and seventies some of my acquaintances decided that they needed to step aside for a time. Before graduation their stories had been shaped by others, but now they needed to shape their own futures. They used the phrase "finding myself" to explain why they were making a stop in their career path. At some point, sooner rather than later, every person and every human institution, especially the church, needs to have a ready and cogent way to state their identity, who they have found themselves to be.

The energy source that powers our journey in life is our identity. We live out of our perception of ourselves. For instance, my wife used to teach middle school. Among her students were a sister and a brother. Their parents had named the girl Angel and the boy Demon. Which do you suppose was the model student and which was always in trouble? Their names had become a summary of their perceived identities. The issue of who we are, who we perceive ourselves to be, presses on us at every twist and turn of our pilgrimage.

With this in mind note that the first public step Jesus makes is to seek baptism. The story of this event is so important that all four evangelists narrate it, but the gospel according to Matthew pulls together most the elements common to all four accounts. So we will explore Jesus' baptism through the lens of Matthew's gospel. His account is found in Matthew 3:13–17.

> Then Jesus came from Galilee to John at the Jordon, to be baptized by him. John would have prevented him, saying, "I need to be baptized by you, and do you come to me?" But Jesus answered him, "Let it be so now; for it is proper for us in this way to fulfill all righteousness." Then he consented. And when Jesus had been baptized, just as he came up from the water, suddenly the heavens were

opened to him and he saw the Spirit of God descending like a dove and alighting on him. And a voice from heaven said, "This is my Son, the Beloved, with whom I am well pleased.

From Matthew we have already heard stories surrounding Jesus' birth, but now the evangelist makes a giant leap through time. We move swiftly from Jesus' infancy to his public appearance at about age twenty–eight or thirty. The setting is the Jordon River as it works its way south through the Judean wilderness.

Here Jesus encounters the wild man of the New Testament, John the Baptist. A polite description would call him an eccentric. But that hardly does justice to John. Jesus said about him, "Truly I tell you, among those born of women no one has arisen greater than John the Baptist." (Matt 11:11)

We know from Luke's gospel that Jesus and John were related. Some have suggested that they were cousins, but in truth we cannot discover the degree of their consanguinity. I think we can say with some justification that they were, at least, acquainted with each other.

John inhabited the harsh Judean wilderness. And he intentionally dressed so as to suggest that he was the successor of Elijah, the first of the great prophets of Israel. Like Elijah he wore a camel skin garment held together with a leather belt, and like Elijah he ate what he could scour out of the desert. The Jewish people at that time would have immediately recognized the connection the first of the prophets and John, the one we can call the last of the prophets. Furthermore, a common belief among those people was that Elijah were reappear to prepare the way for the much anticipated messiah, literally "the anointed one," who they hoped would lead them into a golden age of political power and economic prosperity. We should not be surprised, then, when we are told that all of Jerusalem and Judea went into the desert to meet John.

We today are probably not prepared for the fact that John was a hell's fire-and-damnation preacher. When the religious authorities approached John, he greeted them in this fashion: "You brood of vipers! Who warned you to flee from the wrath to come? Bear fruit worthy of repentance ... Even now the ax is lying at the root of the trees; every tree therefore that does not bear good fruit is cut down and thrown into the fire." (Matt 3:7–8, 10)

Despite the strident preaching many did repent of their sins in preparation for the great thing God was about to do. As a sign of their repentance they were baptized in the Jordon. Scholars discuss the exact significance of John's baptism, but I believe we can call it an act of ritual cleansing marking the beginning of a life newly dedicated to faithfulness to God.

With his background in mind we hear that Jesus makes his way to the Jordon to be baptized by John, and we sense that an enormously important event is about to occur. By being baptized Jesus was stepping into the new reality about which John had been preaching. To put it another way, Jesus the incarnate one was stepping into the new sphere of God's present activity, and Jesus was now about to be the incarnate one *in action*.

At this point we must take a side-step. Jesus has presented himself to John, thereby signifying his identification with the decisive action God is about to accomplish. But the Baptist quickly recognizes a problem with Jesus' intended action, and Christians throughout the centuries have recognized the problem, too. The issue can be stated this way: if Jesus is the Word made flesh, and if John's baptism is a token of the forgiveness of sins, then why should the sinless Jesus be baptized. Why should the inferior baptize the superior? To address this issue Matthew includes a dialogue between Jesus and John. The Baptist speaks, "I need to be baptized by you, and do you come to me?" Jesus' reply has an ambiguous quality about it: "It is proper for us in this way to fulfill at righteousness." (Matt. 3.14–15) He seems to be saying, "This is the right thing to do; this is God's will." The issue still stands, but with that reply John proceeds and baptizes Jesus in the river.

What follows is dramatic indeed. First, the heavens are ripped apart and opened to Jesus. Some medieval art portrays this well. The sky, the heavens, appear as blue cloth with a tear in it. Through that tear extends the hand of God in an act of blessing. The point is, of course, that barrier between the divine and the mundane is opened at the moment of baptism.

Next, the Spirit of God descends like a dove and comes to rest on Jesus. We might well respond by saying, "What an odd occurrence." The meaning of it falls into place when we consider the opening verse of Genesis. In the account of the creation of the world we read that a wind from God swept over the chaos. In Hebrew the words wind and spirit are the same term. And the word swept describes the way a bird flits through the air. When we put this Old Testament material with the Matthew's story we sense that Jesus' baptism is to be understood as a second creation, a new beginning for God's world. The powerful presence of God is at work in a new way, and Jesus is the divinely appointed agent of the new creation.

Then we reach the climax of the story. The divine voice speaks from heaven, "This is my Son, the Beloved, with whom I am well pleased." (Matt 3.17) We can hardly read this without a sense that something extraordinarily significant has happened. Note, moreover, that these words function as a public announcement of what God is doing in and through Jesus.

This single sentence is, as we shall see, is packed with meaning. Consider the first term "son". In the Old Testament the king of Judea was descended biologically from David, the great monarch who united Israel and Judea into a single country, established Jerusalem as the capital city, and placed the Ark of the Covenant on the summit of the city. But the people saw the king in even more portent terms. The second Psalm, which was used during the coronation of the monarch, expresses this understanding: "I will tell you the decree of the LORD: He said to me, 'You are my son: today I have begotten you.'" (Ps 2:7)

The title son stands as the fulfillment of 2 Samuel in which God speaks to David through a dream. God promises to establish David and his descendants as the rulers of God's people, and that the king would the son of god: "I will be a father to him, and he shall be a son to me." (2 Sam 7:14) Over time a term developed to describe this Davidic ruler; the term was "anointed one." In

Hebrew this is Messiah, and in Greek Christ. So in this single word we have reached back into some of the most important parts of the Old Testament, and understand that the term son in all its rich depth is applied to Jesus in his baptism.

When I was in college I spent summers at my parents' home. On occasion someone would call on the telephone, I would answer, and the caller would immediately launch into a conversation assuming it was my father. On the phone he and I sounded alike. Part of the import of Jesus as Son of God is that to listen to him is to listen to the Father. Knowing this piece of his identity empowered Jesus to speak with the confidence and authority of the Son sent by the Father.

Next, the divine voice names Jesus "the Beloved." Perhaps you join me in seeing this as a particularly touching and intimate title. Jesus is the one above all others who receives the love and the commitment of God. Again, we now have another important facet of his identity.

But more remains to be said. The term Beloved has impressive Old Testament antecedents. To explore this we must consider one of the most difficult, even gruesome, stories in scripture. We find it in Genesis as part of the saga of Abraham.

Early in his life God had sought out Abraham and had a solemn covenant with him. God pledged to grant Abraham blessings in the form of land, divine protection, and descendants who would be a means of blessing for the whole world. This promise pivoted on Abraham having a son. Years passed without Abraham and his wife having a child, and they were rapidly growing old and skeptical about God's promise. But the miraculous day finally arrived when Sarah delivered a son. This prompted great joy and happiness, so it comes as no surprise that the couple named their son Laughter, in Hebrew, Isaac.

More years pass and the story takes and unexpected and terrible turn, all of which is narrated in twenty second chapter of Genesis. "Take your son, your only son Isaac, who you love, and to the land of Moriah, and offer him there as a burnt offering on one of the mountains that I shall show you. (Gen. 22:2) The details of the story are narrated for maximum emotional effect. Here is a summary. Abraham has packed his donkey with wood for the sacrifice, and father and son with their servants set out. For two days they journey, and on the third day Abraham perceives the place of sacrifice. He stops and tells the servants to stay, and then he loads the wood on the back of Isaac. At this point Isaac begins to wonder what is in store. He asks his father, "We have wood and fire with us but where is the lamb for the burnt offering?" (vs 7). Abraham calmly replies, "God himself will provide the lamb for the sacrifice." (vs 8) And they walk on.

The story reaches its wrenching climax when Abraham and Isaac reach the designated place. The father builds an altar out of stone, piles on the wood, binds Isaac, and places him on top of the wood. As Abraham has raised the knife to plunge into his son God again speaks, "Do not harm your son, for now I know that you fear me and did not withhold our only son." (vs 12). Just then Abraham spies a ram caught in a thicket, and he uses the animal instead of Isaac as the sacrifice. God reiterates the promise of descendants as numerous as the stars of the sky, divine protection for those descendants, and blessings for and through them. And with that Abraham, Isaac, and the servants return home.

The story leaves most of us silent with horror. What kind of God asks for human sacrifice, and what kind of father would obey? The fact is that in the ancient world child sacrifice was common. If people want to appease and please their gods they sacrificed what they most valued, their children. That practice was part-and-parcel of the culture in which Abraham lived.

So what can we make of this? First, at its most basic level the story says that the God of Abraham does not require child sacrifice and that animals can serve as sufficient substitutes. Indeed, in their later history, God's people developed a special horror of nations and tribes that practices child sacrifice.

Second, we today have lost the sense that God asks the best of us. Our common view is that we can make a token monetary gift and that that suffices. The figure one usually hears is that church members give about one and a half percent of their income—pocket change. We cannot understand this story unless we can imagine that God is so important and that we are so dependent on God that we are obliged to offer our best to God.

Three, Abraham remains disturbingly calm and passive throughout the story. Any parent today, we would like to believe, would angrily balk at such a divine command. Yet throughout the story of Abraham God again and again renews his promise to Abraham of descendants, land, and blessing. Perhaps in this narrative we observe Abraham betting it all on God's pledge. He had done it before. "God will supply" could be a mantra for Abraham throughout his life.

We have probed this story of the sacrifice of Isaac in some detail. Remember this episode begins with God talking about "your son, your only son Isaac, whom you love." Some translations make it overt: your beloved son. Hence, in the baptismal account we sense the depth and power of the title beloved. We are certainly not conjuring up love as warm and fuzzy feelings, but rather love as rock-hard commitment, as promise without compromise. The story portrays love as deeply mysterious and beyond platitudes. Here God, Abraham, Isaac and bound together by covenantal commitment by love.

Further, the church has from its beginning seen parallels between Jesus and the Genesis narrative. For instance, Abraham and Isaac can be analogs for God and Jesus, so that we can understand Jesus as the sacrificial victim offered up to humanity. Any of these comparisons serve as stark reminders that when we understand beloved as an appropriate title for Jesus we have entered a place where love operates at a profound, mysterious level of commitment.

Finally, at this baptism God declares that God is "well-pleased" with Jesus. Some translations say that God "takes delight" in Jesus. We are able to understand the plain sense of this title. Parents easily are well-pleased and delighted with their children.

Again, the phrase has significant Old Testament roots. This time we must turn to the prophecy of Isaiah. The title is prominent in chapters thirty-five through fifty-five. This is a collection of oracles given by a prophet to the Jewish people in exile in Babylon after they have been captured in 587 BC. The prophecies state that God will enable the exiles to return home and again take up their role as God's holy people among all the other peoples of the earth.

As the exiles ponder their future return to Jerusalem God through the prophet tells them that they are to take up a special role and identity for the sake of all humanity. This call is iterated in four passages the scholars refer to as the Suffering Servant Songs. The vocation of God's people will be to take up of work of bearing, carrying, absorbing the suffering of humanity in such a way as to liberate others from their distress. To put it simply, it is a call to sacrifice of self for the sake of others.

Christians have always seen parallels between the figure of the Suffering Servant and the ministry of Jesus, who is the suffering servant beyond comparison. The fourth servant song, for instance, has uncanny parallels with the death of Christ, and thus is always read during the Good Friday liturgy. (Is 52.13–53.12)

Furthermore, the first servant song introduces the servant with these divine words: "Here is my servant, whom I uphold, my chosen in whom my soul delights. (Is 42:1) It continues by describing a gentle yet persistent person whom God has given "as a covenant to the people, a light to the nations, to open the eyes of the blind, to bring out the prisoners from the dungeon, from the prison those who sit in darkness. (Is 4:6–7) Jesus could have adopted this as the mission statement for his ministry as the beloved. In summary, the title the beloved points to Jesus as the servant suffering for the sake of all humanity.

These hugely important passages from the Old Testament serve as roots for Jesus' identity. We can summarize the baptismal story this way. By virtue of his baptism Jesus understood himself as: God's agent gifted with the Holy Spirit so as to empower him to establish the new creation; the Son of God, anointed heir of David, and thus the longed-for Messiah who would lead God's people into the pristine rule of God; the son deeply beloved by God; and the servant who would uniquely complete the vocation of Israel by his sacrifice and suffering. This is Jesus' identity. This is who he was, and it is from this identity that his life took shape.

With that we have completed our exploration of the second phase of the journey of Jesus. Our working assumption is that we can find the life and meaning we need to carry out our journey by examining Jesus' journey. What might our identity be as baptized men and women? What is the spirituality of baptism? What happens when we jump into baptismal waters? These issues we consider in the next chapter.

Questions to assist your thinking about Jesus' baptism:

First, if you were to draw a picture to illustrate a children's Bible what would you include in your portrayal of Jesus' baptism?

Second, in one sentence state your summary of the meaning of Jesus' baptism.

Third, what do you imagine it would be like if your church interviewed John the Baptist to be the priest of your church?

Fourth, how would you react if you were present at Jesus' baptism? What would you see, smell, hear, and feel?

Chapter 4

Swimming in God's Love

ONE GRAY, COLD, AND hazy Sunday I was baptizing a baby boy. Just as I had finished pouring water over his head a beam of sunlight broke through the clouds and shined on the newly baptized child. After the service the grandmother could not get to me fast enough. She exclaimed, "Did you see that? Did you see the way the light landed on him? It's a miracle."

Indeed, a miracle happened that day, but not in exactly the sense she had in mind. Every baptism stands as a miracle of God. In that event the applying of water in the name of the Blessed Trinity God acts in a decisive and momentous way. God rips apart the heavens, so to speak, and comes among us. God grabs the person being baptized and holds them tight. Furthermore, God makes promises to that precious human being: "I know you by name. I will never let you go. You are mine forever. Nothing can wrestle you away from me." Now that *is* a miracle!

But the miracle does not stop there. As if that were not enough in baptism we are joined to the death and resurrection of our Lord. Paul addresses himself to this fact in Romans. In urging the Roman Christians to holy living he poses a rhetorical question: "Do you not know that all of us who have been baptized into Christ Jesus were baptized into his death? . . . For if we have been united with him in a death like his, we will certainly be united with him in a resurrection like his." (Rom 6: 4–5) In baptism we experience a change in our status and position in life; we move from being persons dominated by death to persons who share in the mystery of Christ's death and resurrection. The light of life has broken through and shined upon us.

The church has always used other images to describe the effects of baptism. Sins are forgiven. The baptized becomes part of the church, the living Body of Christ. Baptism serves as our authorization to serve as ministers of the Risen One.

All of this points to the central fact that baptism is the pivot point in the life of Christians. We turn from death and evil to life and salvation. We become a new person in Christ. We live under and by the promises of God.

In most congregations I know a baptism is treated as an important and joyful event. Families gather, special flowers and music are provided, and often a grand meal follows. But to me that seems insufficient. We ought to hire brass bands to march back and forth in front of the church, fireworks should be set off, and during the week to follow people should say to the people they meet, "Did you hear what happened at our church? It was a miracle! A human person was baptized and now shares in the life of the Divine."

From this glorious event, important implications for our lives as Christians and as the church follow. First, in baptism we know who we are. We all know that the issue of identity persistently demands an answer throughout our lives. It is something we seem to need to address again and again. Who am I, really? What makes me who I am? What establishes me as a unique and valuable person? Identity is an existential itch that demands a response.

Furthermore, we live out of our sense of who we are. Our identity is the diving board from which we spring into life. I observe that most people appear to state their identities more in terms of images than in ideas. Have you noticed that once a person has been a Marine they remain a Marine for the rest of life? I suspect that they have in their minds an image or memories of certain events that formed them. Or consider this. I am an Appalachian person. I was shaped by a very distinct culture and it is always with me. When I see those mountains I know I am home.

Let's play a little game. Suppose I give you a sheet of paper and a pen, and I ask you to write all the adjectives that you can quickly think of that describes you. My life would include such items as male, husband, father, citizen, and lover of music. What would be on your list? Given what we have said above "baptized" needs to be at or near the top of that list of identifiers.

Modern church architecture helps teach this. Today as you enter many churches the first thing you encounter is a baptismal font or, even better, a large baptismal pool. The message rings out: to enter into the presence and life of God means being a baptized person.

Many years ago I was confirming a number of persons. Understand that confirmation is a sub-species of baptism; in it a person affirms and renews their baptism and receives the laying on of hands from a bishop to grant the strengthening power of the Spirit. After I confirmed a particular man I anointed his forehead with holy oil in the shape of the cross and looked into his eyes and declared, "You have been anointed with the Holy Spirit and marked with the cross of Christ forever." He broke into a huge smile and said, "Wow!" Indeed. Now he knew where he stood before God and the world. Now his identity was clear.

Second, in baptism I am my noblest and best self. Most of us have an interest in our roots, in our family history. We would like to find someone special or important hanging off our family tree. Then we could proudly point to that ancestor and say to the world, "I have a good and estimable heritage."

Have you even thought of yourself as a sister or brother of Jesus Christ? In baptism, of course, that is who we are. He is the noble and best part of our family and of our own identity. We share in his blessings and reflect the light of his presence. And as we begin to live into that we come to share in his virtues and becomes channels of his blessings to others.

I have served in ordained ministry over forty years, and during that time I seem to have constantly involved in some sort of teaching. One of the bits of wisdom given me through that experience is that people do not learn well when they are shamed or denigrated. Rather, we learn best when we are praised for something done well, when we are listened to, when we are told that we are able to accomplish hard tasks. After a time the student becomes what she or he has been praised for. When a teacher tells a student, "You are a good writer," most of the time that person strives to become an even better writer. Is that not your experience, too?

In baptism we are told that we are precious to God, that God delights in us, and that God desires above all else to bless us. The incarnation says that God has invested all of God's self into this human project.

When I hear that I am energized to live more and more as a brother of Jesus, as a baptized person. I begin to value myself in the way God values me. I become my best self.

On my desk I have my favorite icon, entitled the Holy Kiss. It shows Mary holding the infant Jesus in her right arm, while Jesus has embraced his mother's neck and is kissing her cheek. This icon almost brings me to tears. Here's why. Mary represents humanity, and she clings to Jesus even while he embraces her and kisses her. Mary stands in my stead and in yours. Her son and our Lord holds us close, and eternally and everywhere gives us his holy kiss. In that icon I see my noblest self.

Three, God is at work through the baptized. But before we explore this we need to consider a basic principle of Christian theology, namely, God uses means to do God's work. I once had a parishioner who worked at an extremely challenging job both in terms of intellectual and emotional demands. She once met with me to help her with a persistent question for her. Was this exhausting job a call from God or not? She said, "I wish God would just write the answer in the sky." She, of course, knew that that would not occur. God respects human freedom and will, and would not short circuit those by performing an act that took away choice. As we talked, I sensed that God was supplying an answer if she was willing to hear it. First, she was quite good at her work, and much sought after because of her expertise. And the people she worked with adored her. With shock she told me that they often asked her to pray for them. Those people around her were the means by which God was responding to her query, and she herself was an answer to prayer for the people she served.

Given that we must understand that as the Body of Christ through baptism we become the eyes and ears, the hands and feet of Jesus. The Risen Lord works in us and through us. One of the ways the New Testament expresses this is to speak about spiritual gifts. We can understand these as talents, interests, experiences that God has provided to baptized people so that they can serve, witness, and minister. Sometimes these gifts are described as offices in the church. For example, Paul in I Corinthians 12:28 says that being called to positions in the church are appointments from God. He lists being an apostle (read bishop), a prophet (read preacher), a teacher, a miracle worker, and various forms of leaders and administrators.

In Galatians 5:22–23 Paul describes these baptismal gifts in terms of personal qualities. These include joy, kindness, generosity, self-control, and supremely the gift of love. As you think about Christians you perceive that no one person or one congregations possesses all these gifts. But taken together these people form the Body that fulfills Christ's work.

Late last year I received a call from a member of one of my churches. He thought he might have a call to the diaconate, and he wanted me to hear his story and help in his discernment. In The Episcopal Church deacons are ordained to the work with the poor and powerless of the world; they are servants. Eventually the man called and canceled the appointment saying that he sensed that he was not called to become a deacon. Recently I saw him and he filled out the details. "I thought about becoming a deacon, but the more I thought about the more I saw that God was calling me to something else. My gift is working with wood." He then pointed out six or eight items in the church that he had crafted. All were carefully and beautifully done. Then he offered to give his gift to others in the diocese. "If you know of people who need crosses or kneelers or things like that, let me know and I will be glad to make them." His hands and eyes are means of grace to those around him.

Next, we can trust that God will provide what we need to do what God has called us to do. This stands in contrast to the constant messages of inadequacy that bombard us. Your teeth are not white enough. You are not fit enough. You are not financially prepared for retirement. And each of these implies unwanted consequences: you will be unattractive, you will get sick, you will have to work into your eighties.

We in the church can easily get caught up in this clap-trap. We may not be seriously concerned about white teeth, but we carry the underlying attitude into our churches and lives. I must say I hear this litany too often even in churches. We do not have enough money, enough people, enough energy. We are too old or too young, we do not know the Bible well enough, we are not holy enough, we lack necessary skills. The attitude of deficiency becomes part of our identity. And thereby we and the church sink into the quick sand of scarcity.

In this circumstance we need a dose of baptismal thinking. Since we are baptized into Christ and, therefore, his story is our story, remember that God gave Jesus what he needed to do his work of salvation. If that was true for him, it follows that it will be true for us. Even in his agony in the Garden of Gethsemane when Jesus prayed that he be delivered from his coming death, he was supplied with the courage to be obedient.

And we can again turn to St. Paul for help again. In 2 Corinthians 8:9 he writes these poetic words, "You know the generous act of our Lord Jesus Christ, that though he was rich, yet for your sakes he became poor, so that by his poverty you might become rich." Please note carefully that we the baptized are rich people, rich with empowerment and presence of one who died and rose again.

My wife and I were as poor as church mice in my first year of ordained work. Every penny was given carefully scrutiny. As Christmas approached I began to worry that we might have to skip the holiday that year. Then a parishioner came to me after church and handed me a fistful of Pepsi coupons. She said, "My son-in-law works at the grocery store, and he knows that there is at least one prize among these." She were correct. We won seventy-two dollars, the only time we have ever won anything. Soon thereafter a letter arrived from the bishop. In it was a check for five hundred dollars with a note that simply said, "I thought you might need this." My testimony is that this is the way that it has always been with my family, myself, and all of the churches and the diocese I have served. Always enough to do what we are called to do, that is the promise. God is rich in blessings.

Finally, we can live with hope. I once read a shocking account of events in the Korean War. Some of our soldiers were captured and incarcerated in camps where they were constantly exposed to loud-speaker messages. They proclaimed such things as: your side is losing, many are dying, you will never escape, and no one will rescue you. After two weeks of this some young solders went into a corner, pulled a blanket over their heads, and died. They perished from hopelessness.

Hope is as necessary for human life as food and water. We have a basic and deep-seated need to be able to face the future with some sort of positive expectation. We want they story of our lives to have a happy ending. Without that we perish, sometimes literally.

In baptism we have been buried and raised with Christ. The theological phrase for this is that we live in the paschal mystery. "Pascha" is the ancient name for Easter. We live in ways beyond easy explanation in the dying and rising of Christ. The shape of his story becomes the shape of our story. To put it another way, we can trust that God will be with us in all the death-like places of life, and that God will bring life, peace, and hope out of the death. Please do not misunderstand me. I am certainly not saying that everything will turn out as we want all the time. That manifestly is not true. But I do declare is that God will always work toward life, salvation, and blessing. Just as Jesus prevailed over death, so God will prevail in our lives and the life of the church. We are constantly being challenged to live into the paschal mystery; even in the worst of cases, God is present and will work for the good.

We know the old joke about the man who rode backward on his mule so that he could see where he had been. That past orientation can cause us to view the past as a catalogue of disaster and despair. But the message of the cross, which we will explore in some detail in the next two chapter, says that God is always in the midst of the pain and problems that accumulate around us. But we also know that Easter followed Good Friday, that resurrection overcomes death.

This suggests that we can learn to live beyond fear, worry, and the need to control. We are the baptized. God has joined us to our Lord. The pattern of our lives will always be through the darkness into the light.

My father died suddenly and unexpectedly. My mother had woken to prepare breakfast and found him dead. The doctor who lived next door tried to revive him, but later said that likely my father simply could not have been revived. My brother-in-law called me with the news, and my family and I began the three hour journey back home. When I pulled into the drive way my mother was on the porch waiting for me. She grabbed me and said, "I don't know how anyone can get through this without God." In the midst of darkness came the miracle of light. That is the power and the hope of baptism.

Questions to assist you in thinking about your baptism:

First, do you know the date and place of your baptism? What activities might help you commemorate and celebrate that event?

Second, what spiritual gifts do you have? Take time to write them down. How might God be calling you to use these in new ways both in the church and the world?

Third, what do you most fear? Ponder how being baptized might address and alleviate those fears?

Fourth, can you recall occasions when you have participated in or observed the dynamics of the pascal mystery in action?

Chapter 5, part 1

Shock and Awe

SOME YEARS BACK I was on a pilgrimage in the Holy Land, and had a free afternoon to explore. I walked to the Rockefeller Museum in Jerusalem. At that time they had a special display in the lobby. It was an ancient ankle and foot with a huge nail through the ankle. Recent excavations had uncovered the only known remains of a crucified man, and here it was in a glass case before me. The nail was huge, probably eight inches long, and it had been pounded directly through a bone in the ankle. I hardly knew whether to avert my eyes from this artifact of such a painful event or to indulge my fascination with it. The display pulled me closer to an awareness of the crucifixion of Christ, but also left me in a state of both shock and awe.

In the world of ancient Rome crucifixion represented an extreme form of capital punishment reserved for egregious crimes committed by slaves and other non-Romans. Part of the purpose was to make the victim a cautionary example to others. And, of course, it was intended to impress observers with the might of the Roman Empire.

Today the cross stands as the chief symbol for Christians, but it also becomes a stumbling block for many others. We have to admit that no focus group would recommend such a gruesome object as the selling point for the church. Indeed, the early church seemed to have known this and used other symbols for the Jesus movement, often a fish or a shepherd. The first use of a cross in a church that we know of is in Rome at the Church of Santa Sabina;

the cross was carved into a panel in the door of the church in about 430 AD. Before that it was just too painful and shameful sign for the baptized to use. The analog for us today would be an electric chair or a gas chamber as our common, public symbol, and we know that that just would not work.

Behind these qualms we may have about the object of the cross itself stand a set of questions that we need to be aware of and to address. First, what sort of God is at work here? What God would demand this horrible death as a way of accomplishing God's mission? Second, are we human beings really so sinful, so damaged, that it requires the death of Jesus to deal with us? Three, why is its meaning so ambiguous? As a child in Sunday school, the all-purpose reply to a question we could not answer was, "Jesus died for our sins." Even then I did not clearly know what that meant.

You can see that coming to some understanding of the death of our Lord will require a lot of digging. To capture the richness and profundity of the New Testament's interpretation of Jesus' death I need to ask that you follow me on an extended hike through the scriptures. It will require a bit of patience, but will, I believe, offer you rich rewards. You are free to jump to part four of this chapter if you wish to forego the scripture study, but I recommend that you stick with me.

To begin we need to make a couple of steps backward in Jesus' journey to the cross if we are to comprehend the meaning of these events. A good doorway into this is the first passion prediction. All three synoptic gospels, Matthew, Mark, and Luke, record three occasions when Jesus predicted his coming death. Matthew 16:21 as an instance: "Jesus began to show his disciples that he must go to Jerusalem and undergo great suffering at the hands of the elders and chief priests and scribes, and be killed, and on the third day be raised."

The antagonists who will usher Jesus to his death are listed as the elders, chief priests, and the scribes. The first of this trio formed part of the religious establishment. The elders, for example, made up most of the members of the Sanhedrin, the council that adjudicated the life of Jewish people. Then we meet the chief priests; these men were in charge of the all-important worship of the Temple, where atonement for sins was made. Finally the scribes were charged with the weighty work of interpreting the scriptures; the King James translation of the Bible often called them the doctors of the law.

Along with these we need to mention several other bands of antagonists. First, the Pharisees were a sort of lay renewal movement dedicated to strict observance of the commands of God. At best they were dedicated people, but by Jesus' time they had fallen into inflexible self-righteousness and contempt for those who did not have the ability strictly to observe the law. The Sadducees were a related group distinguished by their denial of a future resurrection for the righteous. Finally, we must add the rich. Jesus' teachings called their lives into question in extensive ways; he manifestly believed that their wealth stood in the way of their entering the kingdom of God.

On the surface these represented the brightest and best of their people. They were respected leaders and their authority was extensive. But Jesus' work of ushering in the reign of God put him at cross purposes with the leaders and ultimately lead to his downfall.

This tension climaxes in the week before Jesus' crucifixion. After entering Jerusalem in a triumphal procession the first item of business was to cleanse the Temple. Matthew records the event.

> Then Jesus entered the temple and drove out all who were selling and buying in the temple, and he overturned the tables of the moneychangers and the seats of those who sold doves. He said, "It is written,
>
> My house shall be called a house of prayer;
> but you are making it a den of robbers." (Matt 21:12–13)

The Temple stood at the center of the spiritual life of the people; it was where they made atonement for sins by their sacrifices offered in the nearer presence of God. Jesus drove out the people who were buying and selling there and upended the tables of the money changers. Because Roman coins had graven images on them and this was forbidden by Jewish law, they had to be exchanged for special Temple currency with no pictures or symbols on them. These special coins were used to purchase the animals used in the ceremonies of cleansing. You may sense that the priests and other officials had set up a nice money-making situation for themselves. In this act Jesus was overturning the corruption at the heart of the religion, and, thus, challenging the leaders at a crucial point of their power and income.

Next he curses a fig tree which had produced no fruit. This was a symbolic act similar to the sort of action used by the ancient prophets. The eighth century BC prophet Amos, for instance, married an unfaithful woman as a living sign of the faithlessness of the people to God. The object of Jesus' curse was to indict the leaders for their lack of ability to produce the fruits of righteousness.

Then follow a series of face-to-face encounters between Jesus and the leaders, who at every step forward to question Jesus' authority. Jesus then lays before them the parable of the wicked tenants. (Matt. 21:33–46). This pronounces a scalding condemnation of the religious leaders, and when Jesus finished the parable we are told that the leaders wanted to arrest Jesus.

More verbal sparring follows, and then we arrive at a shocking climax at Matt chapter 23. We find here a series of "woes" or curses on the scribes and Pharisees. Jesus shames them for locking people out of the reign of God, for loving the letter of the law while missing its spirit, for being blind guides and lovers of public attention, and for their greed and self-indulgence. The Greek word translated as woe suggests a disaster, something painful and horrible to God.

Encounter after encounter follow, and by chapter twenty six we find the chief priests, scribes, and Pharisees secretly plotting to arrest and kill Jesus. Death for Jesus necessarily would follow.

Understanding the meaning of the crucifixion would be nearly impossible without some knowledge of what lead to that event. We have arrived at a place where we can summarize the factors that precipitated his execution. The least that we can say is that issues of power and turf were raised to a crisis level by Jesus' teaching and his parabolic action of cleansing the Temple. For the religious leaders Jesus' questioning of and his attack on their teaching, authority, and character had reached what they perceived as a subversive level. He seemed to undercut the very bases of the religion and of the authority of the leaders.

Moreover, Jesus claimed titles with divine import, such as Son of God, Messiah, and Son of Man (Matt. 26:63–67) For the leaders this was blasphemy and made Jesus worthy of death.

The arrival of the reign of God in the person of Jesus called all the old order, all the powers and authorities into question. Indeed, they needed to be ushered out before the new covenant could come into being. Jesus' mission was to establish a new creation, a new era, and he was willing to put his life on the line to accomplish that.

Questions for discussion:

First, the religious establishment of Jesus' day was divided into sometimes conflicting parties. What do you think was the basis for the conflict with each other and with Jesus? Does this happen in the church today?

Second, what in Jesus' teaching do you think might anger the rich then and today?

Third, what words would you use to describe Jesus' commitment to his mission? What can you learn from this.

Chapter 5, part 2

An Intermission

WE HAVE TRAVELED A distance in our journey to comprehend the
death of Christ and its meaning. We need to stop for a moment to
consider where we stand. At this point three factors are clear. First,
God was at work in the death of Jesus. As always Jesus was func-
tioning as the unique agent of God in the world. Second, the death
of Jesus was necessary. In the first passion prediction we catch
this: "From that time on, Jesus began to show his disciples that he
must go to Jerusalem and undergo great suffering." (Matt 16:21)
The phrase "must go" translates a single verb in the original Greek.
It is a particularly strong verb suggesting the absolute necessity
for Jesus to meet his destiny in Jerusalem. Three, all of this was
understood as the fulfillment of scripture. Matthew's gospel, for
instance, constantly points to Old Testament passages in reference
to the events of Jesus suffering and death. We are to understand,
I believe, that Jesus' crucifixion was not a haphazard event or a
last-minute slap-dash affair, but rather was the careful unfolding of
God's long-standing plan for the salvation of humanity.

At one time I was involved in photography. After trips I
would lay out piles of photos on the floor around me as I tried to
put them in order and write notes on the back of each. Our task
in part three will be akin to that. We will look at ways to put the
meaning and significance of the crucifixion in order, so that we
can come to some understanding of its meaning. In chapter six we
can explore its meaning for our lives.

A discussion question:

Some people are vexed by the idea of the necessity of Jesus' death. For whom was it necessary? Why?

Chapter 5, part 3

Mighty Metaphors

THE WRITERS OF THE New Testament employ many images and metaphors to probe the mystery of the meaning of the crucifixion. I have never found a satisfactory "twenty-five words or less" explanation for it. We are entering, of course, into the realm of mystery where a comprehensive apprehension of Jesus' death is not available to us, but that does not mean that we cannot arrive at some significant understanding by considering carefully the metaphors used in the New Testament.

Our survey of the metaphors and images used by the New Testament writers to explain the crucifixion cannot be comprehensive in a book of this scope. Paul, for instance, uses over twenty-five metaphors to explain the impact of Jesus' death. But we can look at some key passages to sample the rich suggestiveness of these metaphors. This is our task in this part of chapter five.

Mark's gospel uses a single metaphor to interpret Jesus' death. Jesus says, "For the Son of Man came not to be served but to serve, and to give his life as a ransom for many." (Mark 1:45) Jesus serves humankind by being a ransom. In the world of the first century a ransom was a price paid to free someone. We use it in the exactly the same sense when we speak of a ransom paid to free a kidnapped person. The ransom paid by Jesus was his very life. The cross in some way sets people free. We are not told what we are freed from or to whom the ransom is paid, and my personal sense suggests we should not be too eager to answer those questions. We are left to ponder it on our own. Yet, it remains a powerful and life-altering image.

John's gospel takes another approach. In chapter thirteen we come to a passage that marks the beginning of the end for Jesus. He has entered Jerusalem and acclaimed as king. His mission has reached the point that now even Gentiles seek an audience with him. The all-important days of Passover, when the Passover lambs are slaughtered and used in the ritual of atonement for sins, are approaching. John eloquently writes, "Jesus knew that his hour had come to depart from this world and go to the Father. Having loved his own who were in the world, he loved them to the end." (John 13:1) The phrase "to the end" does not refer to chronology but rather to a determinative climax in time. The Greek word for "end" does not refer to a terminus in time but rather to the completion, the fulfillment of time. The thrust of this verse is that Jesus loved just according to God's plan, completely, perfectly, and at just the right time. So we are to understand his passion and death as an act that fulfills and completes God's mission of love.

Just prior to that Jesus speaks to his followers in a suggestive image. In John 12:24 he compares his death to a seed that is planted in the earth and dies, but later bears much fruit. The idea seems to be that his dying will bring life, or that he will live again after this death, or perhaps both.

In John 12:32 Jesus exclaims, "And I, when I am lifted up from the earth, will draw all people to myself." Here we have an allusion to one of the oddest stories in the Old Testament; it can be found in Numbers 21:4–9. It happens as the people of Israel are making their forty year trek across the desert. Because of their murmuring against God and Moses and because of their impatience God sends poisonous snakes to bite the people of Israel. As some of them become ill and die they recognize their sin and ask Moses to intercede for them. God's reply was that Moses should make the image of a serpent sculpted from bronze and mount it on a pole. If anyone was bitten they could look at the bronze serpent and be healed. We could say that this may be a call for people to recognize their sins and face them as a way to find healing. But in the context of John it becomes an image for the crucifixion. In Jesus' death humanity finds the healing God provides.

The metaphors continue. In John 12:28 Jesus says that the cross is the way he will glorify God. Now, this is a bit tricky. In much of the Bible and especially in John's gospel the phrase "the glory of God" refers to God's activity, to what God does, and that activity, in turn, results in the praise and glorification of God by humanity. But the emphasis here lies on the action of God in human affairs. Jesus declares that he will be carrying out the will of God on the cross, and this will be his own praise offered to God. This clues us in that we should see the cross as both crisis and climax. Will Jesus be able and willing to be obey the plan to go to the cross? Can he separate (and that is the root of the word "crisis," to separate) his various motives and emotions so as to love single-mindedly his disciples to the end? It is the hour of decision, and the glorification of God occurs when Jesus' gives his all as an agent of divine reconciliation. As an aside, I hope you see why we take time to explore the details of the biblical texts. It's like digging for gold. A little effort offers great riches.

In John 12:35 Jesus says, "The light is with you a little longer." Jesus refers to an image that has been active from chapter one forward. In the prologue to the gospel we read that Jesus is the light from God that overcomes the darkness of the world. Jesus repeats that claim here. We can hardly miss the implication that it is from the cross that the light of God will shine most brightly. As you consider this, think of all the benefits of light, and apply them to the work of the cross.

Finally, John 12.31 offers still another important metaphor. "Now is the judgment of this world; now the ruler of this world will be driven out." The cross is the decisive battle with the evil one, and Jesus will be the victor. The cross conquers. The cross brings about the ultimate victory of divine love.

So, in just a few verses John lays before us a treasure trove of images. The action of Jesus at the cross is set into motion by the love of God for the world. The result is the healing of humanity and the victory of God over evil. John considers this in cosmic terms and applicable to all people at all time and in all places. The bottom line is that the love of God looks like the cross.

Next we turn to St. Paul in 1 Corinthians chapter eleven. Here we find the earliest account of the Last Supper in the New Testament, likely written in about 54 AD. In this section of his letter Paul is addressing matters of worship. In verses 23–26 he tells us solemnly that he is repeating what has been carefully passed on to him. For our purposes we note two details. First, Paul reminds the readers that at the Last Supper Jesus took bread, broke it, and then said, "This is my body that is for you." (vs 24) The body of Christ crucified on the cross and that body received in the sacrament represent the action of God for the benefit of the world.

Second, Jesus states that his blood effects a new covenant between God and humanity. The blood shed on the cross and the blood received sacramentally establishes a new relationship between God and people. That covenant is worked out on the cross as a new bond between God and humanity for the benefit of all.

This short passage, then, narrates the story of the Last Supper, lays out the benefits of receiving the sacrament, and interprets the death of Christ on the cross. In the crucifixion God solemnly promises to establish a new way of relating to humanity. It is in and through Christ, who gave up his life for the purpose of blessing all people.

Perhaps St. Paul's most profound work is his letter to the Romans. A passage pertinent to our quest can be found in Rom 3:21–26. In this text we find Paul in the middle of presenting his case that all people have sinned, but also that people are set right with God by the gracious will of God manifest on the cross. For Paul the cross, along with the resurrection, stand at the very center of the gospel message. Paul makes use of three images to describe the results of the work Jesus did in his death.

In vs 24 the key word is "justified." A term from the court room, it states that we are pronounced innocent before God. Paul does not explore it any further than that, even though others have tried to say that this term suggests that Jesus was a sort of whipping boy, taking on punishment for human rebellion against God. The wisest course,

I believe, may be to remain close to Paul's narrower understanding and not try to extend the metaphor beyond his usage.

In the same verse we come across the term "redemption." In the world of first century Rome this had a specific meaning. Redemption was the act of freeing a slave, and that usually involved the payment of a fee. On the cross humanity is declared free from slavery. In other places the apostle notes that the freedom won on the cross releases us from bondage to sin, death, the law, and evil.

Finally, in vs 25 Paul declares that Christ's death can be understood as an atonement. This term moves us into the realm of the common ancient practice of offerings of animals to one's god. While strange to our minds, ancient people saw this as part-and-parcel of their lives. They went to the temple of the god about whom they were concerned and gave to the priest an animal, often at great cost to the worshipper. The animal was slaughtered and sometimes burned as an offering to the god, which act was usually understood as a "fine" for sins committed. The result was that the worshipper and the god were considered to be "at one" with the impaired relationship restored. Paul, then, employs this common practice as an image to explain what was accomplished on the cross. Again, we need to avoid pressing the metaphor too far. The apostle does not state to whom the sacrifice of the cross was made or exactly how such an offering changed the relationship between God and humanity. His point is that the crucifixion resulted in a restored relationship between God and God's people; atonement had been made.

Lurking behind these three metaphors lies Paul's larger concern about what he terms the righteousness of God, a central motif in all his writing. He does not use the term in the usual moral sense, that God is somehow innately good. He is asserting, rather, that God is to be understood as righteous because of the way God acts. God is righteous because God acts in the right way. The justification, the redemption, the atonement won by Christ on the cross signals God acting in the right way, and that right way was mercy for humankind. As noted previously, remember that God was acting in and through Christ, not that Christ was doing something to appease God or change God's mind. So, what is the right thing to do? What is the basis of describing God as righteous? Love, of course. God acts in love toward humanity, and for Paul the cross is the supreme sign and proof of God's love.

One of the marvels of medical practice is the MRI. It allows doctors to see inside a person in a detailed way. Paul has given us an MRI of God's mind. The cross of the Lord manifests that God acts in time and space in the person of Jesus, who gave his life as the full disclosure of God's attitude toward humanity. That attitude is love.

As the last item in our quick survey we turn to Hebrews 9:24–28. The book of Hebrews is a sermon-essay to encourage a church that is in danger of losing heart in the face of persecution. The writer's strategy is simply to lift up and celebrate Jesus Christ. One of several ways his does this is to work with the metaphor of Jesus as the great high priest, the one who fulfills and surpasses in every way the priesthood of the Old Testament.

We look at a portion of chapter nine to get a sample of the writer's way of handling the priesthood image. He uses the priesthood and the sacrificial system as described in the Old Testament.

These sacrifices to God had to involve something of great value. What was to happen between God and God's people was far too important to allow for a cheap or ordinary offering. For the people of a largely agricultural culture wealth was calculated by cattle and crops. Furthermore, the offering had to involve blood, because they viewed seat of life as residing in blood. We today still have remnants of that; the American Red Cross calls a donation of blood the gift of life. The result was that a valuable animal had to be given for the sacrifice, and it had to be the best of the flock; no crippled sheep or diseased bulls were allowed. They apparently functioned with a sort of sliding scale; the rich were asked to give a bull, the poor a pair of pigeons. These were handed over to the priests, who had been consecrated for their special work. The animal was slaughtered, and some of the blood was sprinkled on the altar as a sign of life given as an offering to God, and some of the flesh burned so that the smoke ascended into heaven as prayer pleasing to God. This had to occur in the Temple in Jerusalem, the place where God dwelled in a special way. All of this signaled the seriousness of the worshipper concerning his or her relationship with God.

This may be a bit hard for us to understand today. We need to think in terms of virtual rivers of blood and billowing plumes of smoke. An analog today would be for a middle-class person to drive the car to church and hand over the keys; that was the level of sacrifice involved for these ancient people.

The writer of Hebrews assumes the readers know this ancient practice. He then asserts that Jesus is the great high priest who enters the nearer presence of God and offers himself as the perfect sacrifice for the people of God. The writer understand the results of Christ's death in terms of this extensive metaphor.

Three aspects of this imagery need to be emphasized. Christ the great high priest enters the presence of God on our behalf and offers his blood, so to speak. Once again, the cross is perceived to be the means of great blessing for the world, and it is offered freely, graciously, as a gift. That is, God takes the initiative to set things right without prompting or payment on our part.

Second, note that the sacrifice is made in the presence of God. Please do not go further than the writer and assume that the sacrifice is made to God. Rather, understand that God is the witness of the sacrifice, and in that sense validates the sacrifice. Today certain important events have to be performed in the presence of witnesses, who, in turn, sign appropriate documents to attest to their presence. A wedding, for example, requires witnesses to be legal. The witness validates it, and thus makes is true, real, and binding. God witnesses the promise of blessing made in the cross, and thus makes in authentic.

Third, I think it would be difficult for us not to conclude that the cross turns the sacrificial system on its head. Christ in his death was making a sacrifice to humanity as a sign of just how serious and committed God is to God's people. We can say that it is God's appeal to us, a sign and symbol of God's radical dedication to humanity. I am aware that this departs from some traditional views, which I do not deny and continue to value. But I myself find this approach helpful both to my thinking and my prayer. We will consider this further in another chapter.

My wife and I recently had the opportunity to attend an eight course dinner. One wonderful course followed another: moose sausage starters, pea soup, salmon, pheasant and elk and on it went. In this part of chapter five I hope you have experienced this analysis as a grand banquet. It has been a hop-skip-and-jump through the New Testament, and we have tasted only some highlights. Consider our menu: ransom, the glory of divine love, covenant, justification, redemption, atonement, and sacrifice. Even our quick tastings have become a feast, a feast of metaphors of the cross.

Chapter 5, part 4

Analyzing Images

WHEN MY OLDER DAUGHTER was a child she loved to play a game with M & M's. Instead of eating them, she would dump the bag on the floor and then sort the pieces by color, arranging them according to the hues of the spectrum. Then she ate them.

Our last task in this chapter is to sort through all of the images and ideas we have considered. We need to find a way to summarize our work, so that we can in the next chapter consider ways to digest our study in order to live into the cross. We can sort our material under six statements, which summarize where we have been in our journey through the scriptures.

First, the cross represents God in action. We have noted earlier that we will find ourselves bogged down in a moral and theological tangle if we try to state that on the cross Jesus was doing something to God. For example, if we say that Jesus in his crucifixion was appeasing God's judgment, we would quickly conclude that God is morally cruel and crude. We would have every right to ask, "What sort of God demands this horrible death from his son? Does that no make God a moral monster?" In fact, many have come to that conclusion, and have decided that they can live without that God. The antidote to this questionable notion is to be crystal clear that it is God acting on the cross.

Furthermore, if God were demanding this gruesome death of his son that would violate what we know about God's nature in the rest of Bible. Despite some people saying that the God of the Old Testament is angry—when I hear that I am always tempted to ask if that person has actually read the Old Testament—the chief characteristic of God there is, in fact, God's steadfast love, a gracious commitment to humanity so secure that you can bet your life on it. Those ancient authors again and again return to that phrase to explain God's actions.

The approach we must take toward the cross emphatically states that God is acting in and through Christ. Most Christians are familiar with the teaching that Jesus is both fully God and fully man; the early church spent nearly four centuries assiduously working out that doctrine. I have earlier offered my interpretation of that teaching by suggesting that Jesus was the one person fully integrated into God, the one person perfectly transparent to God, the one person whose will and mind were at one with God. When Jesus acts, God acts.

The New Testament itself advances a wonderfully helpful image. In Colossians 1:15 Jesus is describe as "the image of the invisible God." The word "image" in Greek is "icon". If you study icons you know that they are almost always described as windows into heaven. To meditate before on icon is to make your way into the nearer presence of God. So, icons of Christ almost always show his head surrounded by an elaborate halo and the background is decorated with gold leaf in order to suggest that if we look at Jesus we are looking at the divine radiance God. In this book I hope to show that when we study the four major episodes in Jesus' life we most fully understand him as the image and icon of the invisible God.

To behold Jesus in his death is to be confronted with the decisive action of God for the sake of the world. We have to admit that this is counter-intuitive to most of us. When we envision God we often think of power, might, stunning miracles, and people struck dumb with awe. In the past TV stations usually went off the air at 1 AM, and they ended the day with a playing of the national anthem accompanied by a film clip of fighter jets and naval vessels and tanks. We were invited to close the day with the comfortable thought that we are a mighty and powerful people. Our minds tend in the same direction with God, soothing ourselves with the thought that God is all powerful and almighty.

But the cross short-circuits that way of thinking. The God of the cross is hidden by pain and humiliation. The power of the God of the Bible is disclosed in steadfast, vulnerable love. God is revealed by his embracing the problems and pains of life on the cross rather than in power-plays that force us into belief and obedience. The God acting in and through Jesus is both revealed and concealed on the cross.

Second, it follows that God acts in the midst of the problems, pains, and perplexities which plague human beings. This surely has to be one of the most astonishing claims that scripture makes about God and the cross. All the other belief systems of which I am aware—religious and otherwise—offer ways to side-step life's pains or alleviate its perplexity. Some sort of philosophy of life, meditation technique, or wisdom teaching are proposed as answers to life's disasters. Probably the most common attitude is that if we obey God adequately then God will spare us from problems; our obedience will win us a get-out-of-jail card. That puts us in a dilemma, because we can all cite endless cases in which good and godly people suffer.

The cross answers this question: in the midst of the worst that can happen, where is God. The reply manifest in Jesus' death is that God is firmly planted in the midst of everything that can go wrong. If Jesus is God in action in time and space, is this not true? Jesus did not side-step the cross or use miraculous powers to defeat it, rather he embraced it and made it his own. And that fact changes all the ways we understand death and disaster.

We can state this another way. By the cross God makes a stunning act of solidarity with all that it means to be a human being, including even death, our greatest enemy. It signals God's complete commitment to a human race that often rebels, often makes a mess of things, often deals in pain and death.

Years ago a parishioner piloted me in his little airplane. I found it exhilarating to see the familiar landscape of mountains and river from the sky and to swoop around with such ease. Then he said, "Now it's your turn." And with that he took his hands off the controls and his feet off the pedals. Now I knew nothing about flying; I was just out on a lark. I grabbed the controls and put my feet on the pedals, and quickly discovered that I could not control the plane. We bobbled, slowed down and speeded up, twisted this way and that. In panic I said, "Vince, I can't do this," and he took back command of the plane. Ever since that day I have had a deep respect for pilots. I have been in their seat, and know what it means.

Being there, experiencing the difficulties, sharing the ups and downs makes all the difference. From the cross God eternally says: I know. I share the difficulties and disasters that drain us of life. I am there with you always. That is how committed I am to you!

Third, from the cross God attacks evil. After watching an episode of the evening news it would be hard not to conclude that there is something terribly wrong with us and our world. In thirty minutes we observe a parade of human misery and disaster, much of it of our own making. We can't take our eyes off the screen even while we can hardly bear to watch.

Some might rightly ask: so what is God going to do about it. Injustice and pain appear to be rampant and unrestrained, and we might conclude that God has left us to our own feeble devices. The cross, however, is God's response. The cross represents God's decisive attack against evil.

In speaking of the fullness of life in Christ, the writer of Colossians says in 2:15, "He disarmed the rulers and authorities and made a public example of them, triumphing over them in [the cross]." The imagery here recalls the roman triumphal procession. When the armies of Rome conquered others they took hostages, especially generals and rulers, put them in chains and marched them on foot through the streets of Rome. It was an exercise in public humiliation for the defeated and a sign to the citizens of Rome that they were the rulers of the world. So in the cross God in Christ engaged the forces of evil that are active in injustice, pain, humiliation, loneliness, and failure, all of which Jesus endured during his crucifixion. And in that act God in Christ was absorbing and embracing all of those dehumanizing and death-dealing powers, thus robbing them of their power.

I am an avid baseball fan. One of the many pleasures of that game is watching a wily batter handle anything that the pitcher can throw him. He takes all the fastballs, curves, and cutters and comes out the victor, making his triumphal trot to first base. On the cross, God takes all that evil can throw, but is never overcome or defeated. God on the cross is the victor.

Part of the job of any leaders is to deal with conflict and anger. One of my seminary teachers spent the large part of an afternoon explaining "sacrificial leadership." The trouble ceases, he said, when the leader makes the dissension and antagonism his or her own. An effective leader knows that there are occasions when he or she should just accept the blame for a problem, or apologize to someone who is hurt and angry. "I sometimes make mistakes. I am probably to blame. I am upset that you were hurt. I apologize." Such statements by a leader defuses the blame, the anger, the evil, and in doing that healing takes place. Sacrificial leadership imitates what Jesus did on the cross.

Four, the cross demonstrates God's commitment to humanity. Whenever I review the narrative of the passion and death of our Lord, I am always astounded to see again what human beings are capable of doing. We have in Jesus the best human being who ever lived, and he was brought down by the fear and jealousy of religious authorities and the deceit of one of his inner circle. When he was arrested his was denied by Peter, the chief of the apostles, and the rest of the disciples simply deserted him. Bluntly stated, the agents of evil in the passion story are human beings. When we pose the question of what we did to the best of men, the answer is that we killed him.

In light of all that we might ask some hard questions. Is there a line in the sand that if violated God would throw up God's hands and say, "I've had enough of these people"? In humanity's relationship with God is it possible that we could impose so much on God's mercy that God would just walk away from us? Can we push God too far?

The answer of the cross is stunning. There is no line in the sand, no way we can go too far, and no way we can push God's mercy over the limit. We have already done on that on the cross. And yet Jesus took up the cross and bore all the ignominy of it, saying only, "Forgive them."

The cross, then, becomes the ultimate sign of God's loyalty and allegiance to humanity. In a passage of great beauty Paul sums it up. "I am convinced that neither death, nor life, nor angels, not rulers, nor things present, nor things to come, nor powers, not height, nor depth, nor anything else in all creation, will be able to separate us from the love of God in Christ Jesus our Lord." (Romans 8:38–39)

The nearest we come to sharing in this committed love and loyal allegiance is found in marriage vows. Two people face each other, hold hands and pledge life-long faithfulness to each other no matter what, in good time and bad, in wealth or poverty, in sickness and health. Many marriages in our culture come to end, but over my thirty years of parish ministry I have often been astounded at how couples manage to fulfill those vows, standing by each other in terrible times. For example, I remember a parishioner who was slipping away after a long struggle with cancer. In the final days her husband did not leave her side, even sleeping on the hospital floor beside her at night. When I see that sort of love I see people sharing in the eternal and radical commitment of God to humanity.

Fifth, the cross reveals that God takes all possible measures to embrace us. By now we should be able to sense that the story of the cross pushes us to the outer limits of our ability to imagine the extent of God's faithfulness to us. What more could God have done?

All of us collect various bits and pieces of data, and use that to draw a conclusion. "Look at those dark clouds. The wind is picking up. I suddenly feels cool. I bet it is going to rain." We apprehend truth in the particular and the specific. So it is with the cross. In that particular time and place, in the unique person of Jesus, God was definitively revealing how far God would go to embrace us in mercy and blessing. It had to be that specific to be convincing.

Some years back I had to be out of town for an extended period and I left my springer spaniel Lizzie with a friend. I had been gone a few days when I received a panicked call from one of my staff. It was a Saturday and he had been walking past the office and found Lizzie sitting by the front door not wearing her collar. I made some quick calls to get her back to her dog sitter. Earlier that day the sitter had left her house to do some chores. Lizzie opened the back door of her house, and then unlatched the gate of the fence, and began the two mile journey across Helena to the office. How she did that remains a mystery to me. But this I know. She did to be near me. If my dog does that, imagine how it is with God.

Sixth, the cross means love. The meaning of that word love can be elusive, because we use it in so many ways. It runs from "I love chocolate" to "I love my spouse." But I would observe that most of the time we use it to refer to a feeling, a much-to-be desired warm and pleasant feeling. Years ago a popular children's story called this sort of love "the warm fuzzies."

The cross speaks of another sort of love. Cruciform love is the crystal clear and rock hard commitment of God for all that God has created, including and especially humanity. God has vowed to bless the world, to work for our healing and salvation, and to reconcile the whole world to God's self. God's love is not composed of something as fleeting and capricious as feelings. God's love says that God is always and forever pledged to seek and to endow us with divine favor.

I noted earlier that the chief characteristic of God in the Old Testament is a single Hebrew word usually translated as "steadfast love." Underline the word steadfast. Think of synonyms for it: faithful, loyal, constant, unfaltering, devoted, steady, and reliable. You get the idea.

That virtue of steadfast love finds its fulfillment in the events of Jesus' suffering and death. There the utter allegiance of God to us, despite everything painful and horrible that could happen to Jesus, stood firm and unwavering. That is the meaning of love.

One of the "must-see" sights in Florence, Italy is the Church of Santa Maria Novella. It houses many delights and treasures, but surely the greatest is Masaccio's fresco of the Holy Trinity. It would have been the first thing you would have seen if you entered the main door during the Renaissance. It is quite large and requires that you look up to see it. In his extended arms God holds Christ hanging on the cross with a small dove of the Holy Spirit moving from God to Jesus. It is as if God is holding up the crucified Lord for all to see, extending the cross for all people to behold. It is hard to move away from this astonishing painting. God seems to be saying, "This is who I really am. You will not know me apart from the cross. Behold my love for you."

Some questions to spark your thinking:

First, if Jesus were physically present today, how do you think he would most unsettle us in the way he unsettled the scribes and Pharisees? Why?

Second, of all the New Testament metaphors used to make sense of the cross, what is the one you find most meaningful? Why?

Third, how would you explain to a child the phrase "Jesus died for our sins"?

Four, how would you describe God's love to a person unfamiliar with that concept?

Chapter 6

Seven Blessings of the Cross

SOME YEARS BACK I was scouring around in a gift shop in Jerusalem. I came upon an item that immediately captured my attention. It was a cross carved from olive wood about eight inches tall, and attached to the bottom of it was what appeared to be handle. I found it attractive and interesting, but I was not certain of its use until sometime later when I saw a photo of an Orthodox bishop blessings his people. In this right hand he held a cross similar to the one in the gift shop. When I bless people I simply use my right hand to make the sign of the cross, but he was using an actual cross to bless people.

Christians understand the cross to be one of the great and definitive graces from God to humanity. God literally blesses the whole creation through the cross.

In this chapter we will explore the ways in which the cross blesses us in radical, profound, and life-changing was. We will consider seven blessings bestowed on us by Jesus' death on the cross.

The first blessing of Jesus' crucifixion is this: the cross delineates God's reply to the problem of pain. On All Saints' Day, Nov. 1, 1755 while many of the citizens of Lisbon, Portugal where in church a devastating earthquake struck the city. Estimates suggest that it may have been as much as a nine on the Richter scale, and it destroyed most of the city and surrounding areas. The loss of life was staggering. Because of the rise of newspapers and their ability to communicate quickly this event became the talk of Europe. And philosophers raised this issue: how can a God who is said to be good allow such a tragedy. Why does God allow such horrors to occur?

In the twentieth century C.S. Lewis wrote a book addressing this issue from the perspective of a Christian. He entitled it *The Problem of Pain*. This term will be what I use here.

The question persists, and most of us are hard pressed to offer an answer. Refugee children die. Why? People are mowed down by crazed shooters. Why? Good, moral people waste away from cancer. Why? These examples give only a sampling of the problem of pain.

Many philosophies and faith systems lay before us possible answers. For example, if you are able to practice detachment you can live beyond the problem. Or, some would say that pain is an illusion of the mind, and that proper thinking will clear up the issue. Or, life and the problem of pain are without meaning, and, therefore, we need to accept that fact and soldier on through life. Or, simply try to drown the issue with entertainment, recreation, and alcohol.

Moreover, Christians reply with some other attempts. For example, over my three decades of parish work I visited many hospitalized people, and I heard these attempts to tackle the problem of pain. "It must be the will of God. I do not understand it, but I will trust that God wants this for me." Or, "this must be punishment for sins. I don't know what they are, but that has to be reason I am here in pain in this bed." Or, "I can't get my mind around it, but I am willing to let it go into the hands of God." These replies have merit because they offer the comfort of making sense of pain and tragedy, but if you are like me you do not find them satisfying. They seem like attempts to stumble your way through a pitch black room.

We have come to the end of the rope in trying to make sense of the pain, tragedy, disease, and death. The above responses have value, but they are like applying salve to third-degree burns.

When we have reached an intellectual and emotional dead-end then we finally find ourselves in a position where we can seriously hear the message of the cross.

The value of the cross in the midst of tragedy lies in its power to draw us back into the very heart of God. The key to unlocking the meaning of the death of Jesus is remembering that God is at work in a decisive way on Calvary. Two factors come into play here.

First, Jesus knew about his destiny on the cross, and he chose to do it, albeit reluctantly. He struggles with his impending death, but in the end submits to its necessity. In Jesus doing the work of the cross, all of humanity is encompassed in his obedience, and, therefore, into his saving work.

Second, we see God's heart in Jesus' graceful and non-violence acceptance of the cross.

"Father, forgive them; for they do not know what they are doing" (Luke 23:34). The deadly cycle of anger and vengeance is broken on the cross, and in that we can recognize the God who always seeks reconciliation rather than punishment.

As we contemplate the cross in light of the problem of pain, two important and life-altering conclusions appear. First, God embraces all the pain of the world in Jesus' passion and death. If God acts in the cross, then God is making tragedy and suffering God's own. For instance, the medical advice for snake bite used to be to cut a cross through the skin over the bite, and then suck out the venom. God does just that in Jesus' acceptance of pain in that God has taken it upon and into God's own self.

Just consider what Jesus endured. He experienced the apparent failure of his mission, a kangaroo court, desertion by his followers, gross distortion of his words and works, public humiliation, weakness, pain, mockery, grief, and a slow death. Just about everything that could go wrong did. And that God owned in and through the cross.

But the blessed result is our freedom. We do not need to carry the burden of guilt, fear, pain, failure. We do not have to be loaded down with the perception that we are merely specks of dust blown about by the winds of indifferent fate.

One summer when I was in college I worked for a wholesale plumbing and electrical company. Part of my duties included delivering purchases to various job sites. The truck I used had welded to its side L-shaped steel bars on which I loaded iron pipe used for water and gas lines. One afternoon, I was forced to make a sudden emergency stop, and all of the pipe slide off the racks and scraped against the pavement. The threading on the end of many of the pipes was ruined by its impact on the street. I felt guilty, incompetent, and ashamed. I delivered the order, went back to the shop, and told my boss what had happened. "We all make mistakes. Don't worry about it," he said. He was willing to bear the complaints of an angry customer and the cost of replacing the ruined pipe. And I was free. God works the same way to set us free.

Thus, the cross reveals the depth of God's commitment to humanity. In all of the relationships that we can think of we know that certain actions can bring an end to that relationship. In a marriage a solemn pledge of life-long faithfulness is made by two persons in the presence of God, but that relationship can be broken if one partner commits adultery or physically abuses the other. All relationships have an implied limit, and if one partner violates that limit the bond is broken. All partnerships involve a contract or covenant or an understanding, and if one party violates the understanding enough times, the connection dissolves. We understand this almost at an instinctual level. All human bonds are fragile and can be shattered as the result of certain actions or words.

The cross, however, states: there is no line escape clause in the contract, no dissolvable covenants, no escape clauses. The cross declares that nothing can destroy God's total and complete commitment to us. Remember what human beings did to Jesus, and yet he remained faithful. In the face of all woe we pitched at him, his response was, "Father, forgive them." Jesus' response to the cries of "Crucify, crucify him" was perfect commitment to humanity and to God's mission.

We become recipients of this breathe-taking bond in the sacraments. Holy Baptism promises that we are daughters and sons of God always and forever, because we have been joined to the death and resurrection of Christ. In Holy Eucharist Christ gives us his own Body and Blood despite what we may have said or done.

This sort of commitment is described by a certain term in the Christian vocabulary: love.

This sort of love is not concerned with feelings or desires, but with the attitude that chooses to act for the blessing of the other. What we know of God is exactly that God's deepest commitment is to bless us. Note carefully these words of St. Paul. "I am convinced that neither death, nor life, nor angels, nor rulers, nor things present, nor things to come, nor powers, not height, or depth, nor anything else in all creation, will be able to separate us from the love of God in Christ Jesus our Lord." (Romans 8:38–39) God's committed love is solid enough for us to build our lives on it.

Many years ago I worked as a seminary chaplain in a major hospital. On my assigned ward was a woman in her thirties. I do not now remember her diagnosis, but I do recall that she was confined to her room for several weeks. During some of our conversations she revealed that her husband had not been to visit her. I asked her why. "He doesn't like hospitals," she replied. He lacked a basic grasp of commitment and love for his wife. The issue was not what he disliked, but rather what she needed. But we all know that we often miss the point and fall far short of love for God and neighbor. But God does not. The cross stands as the stunning symbol of God's commitment to us.

The cross blesses us with a second existential truth: no good thing happens apart from sacrifice. Let me offer an example in reverse. I have always enjoyed camping ministry and am committed to it. I think I have not missed some time at church camp for over thirty years. One summer I got a phone call in my cabin at about 11 PM. One of the campers was ill. I went to his lodge, and found the other campers there in a turmoil. "We can't stand that sound anymore," they said. This little camper was using his finger to provoke vomiting. He hoped that would relieve his stomach ache. I talked with him, and learned two things. First, he had had five hamburgers for dinner that night. That explained the stomach ache. But he also told me that when this happened at home, he would wake up his dad, who would always tell him, "Go away and stick your finger down your throat." Clearly the father did not want to be bothered.

Those of us who have been parents know that it involves lots of sacrifice, including getting up in the middle of the night to care for a sick son or daughter. And it never stops. Parenthood is a call to constant giving, caring, and sacrifice.

But just when being a father or mother becomes burdensome we remember that our parents did the same for us, otherwise we would never have survived. When I graduated from college many decades ago one of my classmates had removed the tassel from his mortarboard and replaced it with a price tag reading "$40,000." I found that funny, but it also reminded me in a very pointed way of what my parents had sacrificed to send me to an expensive private college.

Sacrifice is called for not only in families but also in the church. I spend a lot of time with vestries, which are the elected lay people who along with the rector form the governing body in every Episcopal congregation. Some of the new vestry members sometimes tell me, "I had no idea how much time and energy this would take." Churches do not thrive unless people are willing to give away their time, energy and financial resources for the sake of Christ and the congregation.

This brings us to the issue of the nature of sacrifice. In some communities the United Way asks people to give a portion of their income to the work of that important organization. Normally the employer simply deducts it from a paycheck, and it is usually a very small percentage of the salary. I support the United Way, but we must surely acknowledge that this is not sacrifice, but rather acquiescence to a modest request.

Let me offer a three-part definition of sacrifice, First, to sacrifice is to give away part of yourself freely for the benefit of another. Time, talent and energy clearly constitute part of ourselves, but money does as well; I had a mentor who called money "minted self."

Second, sacrifice involves some pain. It has to hurt in some sense, and cannot be casual or easy. Throwing your pocket change in the Christmas kettle cannot be called sacrifice. It is a nice thing to do and makes you feel good, but it is not a sacrifice. Contrast that with the above instance of sending a son or daughter through college. There used to be a slogan that went, "If you haven't given until it hurts, you haven't really given." Surely Jesus' offering of himself on the cross drives home this point.

Three, sacrifice grows out of gratitude. The virtue of gratitude does not come naturally to human beings, but rather we have to be taught it. Again, parents know that they must teach their children to say "thank you." Gratitude begins to grow strong when we realize that all the blessings of life are gifts. All of life is an experience of grace. When we have heard and digested the story of Jesus we begin to be captured by gratitude in response to the fact that Christ reveals the God who gives and gives and gives in order to bless us. Both Morning and Evening Prayer in the *Book of Common Prayer* end with this:

> Almighty God, Father of all mercies, we your unworthy servants give you humble thanks for all your good and loving-kindness to us and to all whom you have made. We bless you for our creation, preservation, and all the blessings of this life; but above all for your immeasurable love in the redemption of the world by our Lord Jesus Christ; for the means of grace, and for the hope of glory. And, we pray, give us such an awareness of your mercies, that with truly thankful hearts we may show forth your praise, not only with our lips, but in our lives, by giving up ourselves to your service and by walking before you in holiness and righteousness all our days." (p 101)

This beautiful prayer says it all. God is the source of all blessings and the energy behind our sacrifice.

Look around. Is it not true? Nothing good happens without sacrifice.

For Americans it would be almost impossible to imagine our country or the presidency without reference to George Washington, who was in many ways the father of the United States.

He was not eager to become the first President, but he also knew that the infant country would not survive and thrive unless he accepted that high office. At the end of his second term he gave notice that he intended to step down, return to Mount Vernon, and allow someone else to assume his position. When King George heard this news he said, "If he does that he will be the greatest man in the world." He could hardly imagine someone willingly sacrificing power, prestige, and honor. But it was just this sort of sacrifice that insured the continuing life of the United States.

What might happen to us, the church, and the world if we could understand the sacrificial nature of God's love? What would happen if we began to invest ourselves in the business of sacrifice?

Three, the death of Jesus on the cross demonstrates how valuable we are to God. We seldom invest much time or energy in exploring the deep and hidden parts of our lives. Most of us are caught up in keeping up with our calendars and with completing our "to-do" lists. Perhaps we avoid that probing exploration out of fear of what we might discover in the corners and crevices of our hearts.

Deep inside, I believe, lie some profound needs and desires that drive us, motivate us even in ways of which we are not aware. These needs function as powerfully as our requirements for food, water, and air. We long for release from our shame at the damage we have done to self and others, at the intentional wrong we have committed out of anger or self-interest. We have thirst for the sense that our lives have meaning and significance, that we are valuable people who can make a difference. We yearn for hope, for the belief that life is worth living. And we dream for being people who are known, valued and accepted, despite our sins and problems. Deep down, hidden away lies an emptiness that demands to be filled.

The Christian gospel addresses just this need. Paul makes as case for this in his little letter to the Philippians. He appears to be quoting an early hymn, which declares that Jesus gave up his divine powers and prerogatives, emptied himself, became human, and died on the cross (Phil. 2. 6–8). Does this not declare just how valuable we are to God in Christ? Did not Christ give up all for our benefit? Does not the cross show how far God will go to be bound to us? Can you think of any other instance that surpasses this?

We can look at this in another way. Ancient people depended on crops, rain, and family just as we do. But they also knew they lived a tenuous world where food, water, and children might or might not appear. And they, furthermore, sensed that their actions and attitudes could affect their lives. They realized that they needed to be in the good graces of their gods. They knew that they needed to be at one with divine powers. In short, they needed to make atonement for their mistakes, errors, and sins. Their job was to sacrifice to their gods in order to gain divine favor. The way of the cross demonstrates that God takes the initiative to bless us and, in a sense, make the supreme sacrifice to win our love.

The great good news of the cross is that God has taken steps to put things right, and that God does that because we are infinitely valuable to God. This brings two truths into focus. First, in every area of life we assume that we have to act to set things in order, and our religious beliefs tend to coincide with that. We should seek God, we say, by behaving in good ways, and then perhaps God will reward us. The gospel declares the astonishing fact that God has reversed this pattern. God has already acted to make the whole creation new, and God's motivation is God's great desire to be with us and bless us. That's how valuable we are.

Moreover, those hidden desires and longings tell us of our need for God. God uses even these dark yearnings to put us on the path to relationship with God. Augustine of Hippo wrote this pithy line: we are restless until we rest in you, O God.

Our task consists in allowing these truths to trickle down into our hearts. The ideas need to become images, attitudes, and actions. In this way that empty place at the center of our lives is filled. We absolutely need to know how valuable we are to God in order to live.

Years ago, a woman along with her sister and father began to attend church. People welcomed them and I found them interesting and kind-hearted members. I noticed that the woman had not been in church for about a month, and so I decided to call on her at her home. As soon as she saw me at the door she burst into tears. "God can never forgive me for what I have done," she sobbed over and over again. She sat on the couch with her head in her hands and with tears dripping on the floor. I tried to tell her about the mercy and forgiveness of God, all based on how much God treasures us. She continued with the tears and her mantra, and finally I simply left her weeping in her living room. I never did find out what she had done, and she never returned to church. This illustrates the power the deep places of our lives have over us, and this insists that we need to know how much God values us.

The cross blesses us in a fourth way in that it causes us to interpret the pain of the world in a new way. In the third grade my teacher asked me why I made so many mistakes on my arithmetic problems. I told her I could not see the board. I note went home with me that day, and a visit to the optometrist followed. On the way home from his office with my new glasses I was stunned. I could see the individual leaves on the trees and single blades of grass. I saw the world in a new way.

The cross allows us to see the pain of the world in a new way. The death of our Lord reveals that all the despair, distress, and death of the world are caught up into the heart of God. Therefore, pain is not and cannot be the last word on life. Jesus died in distress and alone. That fact has become part of God's story.

In the last church I served my predecessor remained in the community, but shortly after my arrival he died of a heart attack. The staff of the hospital told me later that on that morning of his death he seemed to be struggling until his sister arrived. As soon as she touched his hand, he passed away. Don't we all fear loneliness, especially at the time of death? The fact of God acting in the cross says to me that God knows loneliness, and, therefore, I am not alone in my aloneness. I see it in a new way.

One Sunday morning a fellow bishop and I were walking to church through the streets of London. We came across a homeless man, curled up and sound asleep in a doorway. His dog laid with him. Now, I am a lover of dogs, and perhaps attribute to them more intelligence and heart than they, in fact, have, although I doubt it. That dog touched me deeply. "At least, he is not alone," I said to myself. It makes a difference to me to know that Jesus had not place to lay his head, and that on the cross he lost literally everything. God knows homelessness and loneliness, and the cross bespeaks the truth that God finds a way to be with us—maybe even in a dog.

As we look into ourselves and out into the world, we might well conclude that God has left the scene. I encounter folks all the time who seem to believe that. But if we see ourselves and our world through the cross, we can believe that God has been here and that God knows the deepest depths of our pain.

When I drive through Butte, Montana I sometimes pass a building with a big neon cross on it. The sign says "Gospel Mission," and it marks one of that city's major agencies of helping the homeless and hungry. The death of Jesus *is* God's gospel mission to us. God knows we need help, because God has seen it all on the cross. And that changes everything.

Five, the cross calls us to engage in the problem of pain. I was walking to lunch recently when I passed what appeared to be a homeless woman. I asked, "How are you doing?" She replied, "I'd be better if I had some place to live." I didn't stop, but rather stepped away as quickly as I could. I was hungry, and that's what I wanted to deal with, not this woman's painful problem. I had been given an open door into sacrificial service, and I said, "No thanks. Lunch is waiting."

By virtue of our baptism we share in the dying of Christ. We die to self in order to live more deeply into the resurrection of our Lord. We walk the path he walked, and we imitate what he did.

Jesus and the twelve apostles were on their way to Jerusalem, and Jesus takes them aside to tell them again that he will meet his destiny in Jerusalem, that he will be handed over to death.

In an example of totally missing the point, James and John had their mother ask a favor of Jesus: when you establish your kingdom, can my sons be your vice-kings. Jesus turns to the two brothers and poses a question to them: can you drink the cup I am about to drink. Boldly they answer: we can do that (Matt 20:17–22).

This little episode demonstrates where the disciples of Jesus should be. To share in the cup at the Eucharist means we share in the cup of his sacrifice for the sake of others. To put it bluntly, to be involved with the crucified Jesus is to jump into the pain of the world with both feet.

In the world I grew up in the church was concerned with the "deserving poor." The problem with that lies in assumption that we get to say who is deserving. But Jesus did not work with people in this way. The God of the cross shows that God is not judgmental about who is deserving or not, but rather on the cross gathered to God's self all the painful consequences of sins, errors, mistakes, injustice, and callousness. We need, therefore, to proceed in the same manner. Judging is not our job. We, like Jesus, walk with people in pain and we embrace their suffering.

I still meet people who assume that alcoholism represents a moral failure, weak discipline, lack of will. But for followers of the Jesus of the cross these assumptions are not relevant. People whose lives and families are being destroyed by alcohol or any drug demand compassionate, non-judgmental action.

Another way we side-step involvement is by studying and thinking about a problem, and then setting up a committee to work on it. Of course, understanding an issue is a necessary prelude to action, but we can easily get caught up in talk and analysis. My experience is that Christ has a way of slapping us in the face and saying, "Do something, do almost anything about that." And act we must.

Finally, we must caution ourselves about the trap of serving as a means of making ourselves feel good. We share in the pain of the world because Jesus calls us to it, not because it generates a warm glow. That warm glow can quickly become mere religious self-indulgence.

I recently attended a meeting at Christ Church Cathedral in Cincinnati. We left the meeting as the winter darkness was falling, and noticed a gathering of street people in one of the public areas of the church. Every Tuesday night a group of members use some of the offerings given by other members to prepare and serve a gourmet meal to anyone who presents themselves. The food is hot and there's lots of it, and it is served on the cathedral's best china at no cost.

That's what I'm talking about

The sixth existential blessing is: the cross calls us to care for the earth. Some years back I was in Italy studying sacred art. I came across a fresco by Giotto. It portrays Jesus dying on the cross. The ground is brown and devoid of vegetation, and the sky is pitch black. Around the Jesus are angels swirling in paroxysms of grief. All the universe, heaven and earth, are caught up in the anguish of Christ's death.

Giotto must have known Matthew's account of the crucifixion. As Christ dies the sun seems to go dark and the ground quakes. The earth and sky are caught in a grief as deep as that of Jesus' family and friends.

The Bible always understands that nature is involved in the story of salvation. In the creation story in Genesis chapter three the world reverberates with the fall of humanity. The man and woman seek to be like gods by attaining the knowledge of good and evil; that results in the fall of the whole world. Snakes are now doomed to crawl in the dust and to be at odds with humanity. The ground now will produce thistles and people will need to work hard to produce crops. And in the end, people die and return to the dust of the ground.

If we fast-forward to the end of the Bible, we catch a glimpse of creation restored and renewed. In the last chapter Revelation heaven flows with the water of life, which nourishes the tree of life, the fruits of which will heal the nations. God shapes a new creation and Eden is restored.

The point is that if we share in the cross we will seek to care for the earth. It, too, is part of God's creation and shares in the salvation wrought on the cross. For us, even ecology is cruciform.

If we share in Christ's death via our baptism, we also share in the sacrificial work of caring for creation.

We know well enough what will be required of us if we are to practice this cruciform ecology. Examples are not required. What we do need, however, is a good, compelling reason to do the work required. Developing alternative sources of energy, recycling, and reclaiming polluted ground will require that we sacrifice some of our financial resources, but in comparison with the cross that seems a small price to pay.

For example, The Episcopal Church observes the three days before the Feast of the Ascension as rogation days. This coincides with the planting of fields in many parts of the world. Prayers for fruitful seasons and for faithful stewardship of the earth are used. In England priests used to walk of the geographic boundaries of the parish reciting psalms and prays for the earth. Because we do not generally have geographically defined parishes in this country, the practice of "beating the boundaries" is not usually practiced here. But I can imagine the effect it would have on people and priest as they traced the periphery of the parish, praying as they walked. They would feel and smell the earth, they could look at the green of leaves and grass, and they could watch people laboring in fields. How could they not sense the ways in which they were intimately connected with the earth and sky? How could they not conclude that Christ's death was for the sake of the whole creation? How could they not offer a sacrifice of praise and thanksgiving for the earth for which Christ died?

Seven, we are given the opportunity to make cruciform choices. We have all heard people say, "I guess this is my cross to bear." They are usually commenting on some persistent irritant in their lives, anything from fallen arches to grouchy in-laws. But that way of thinking does not catch what Jesus had in mind when he called us to share in his sacrificial life and ministry.

The opportunity to bear the cross is not so much something foisted on us as it is our Lord inviting us to participate in the reign of God. It comes to us as call and choice.

Jesus' call asks us to put into action our interests, abilities, and experiences as disciples. We, of course, have the right not to respond, but we also have the happy option of putting ourselves into the service of our Lord. For instance, I love baseball, but am too awkward and old to play. I am pretty sure that I do not have a call to coach a youth baseball team. But I do love to read and have spent a lifetime doing that. I think I could be a good leader of a book group. The call blesses us with the occasions to harness the gifts we have in order to offer them as a sacrifice and praise and thanksgiving to Jesus.

Choice can, however, present us with a knotty problem. God has gifted us with the invaluable ability to make choices, and God respects that. If God were consistently to force us into certain ways of acting or thinking our ability to think and to exercise our wills would soon wither and die. So, we live in a reality in which we always have choice.

But we tend to complicate that with the distinction of what we want and what we are called to do. All of us have a tendency to collapse that distinction. For example, I was once considering buying a sports car. I was discussing this with a friend, who said, "Go ahead. God wants you to have that car." That was just what I wanted to hear. But I knew deep down that purchasing the car had little or nothing to do with following Christ's call in my life; it represented a desire, not a need or an occasion for service.

If you make a pilgrimage to Jerusalem one of the "must do" events is walking the Via Dolorosa, the Way of the Cross. You wind through the streets of the city stopping at each of the four-teen stations, each marking an event in Jesus' journey to the cross. Sometimes people even carry a large wooden cross with them. You make your way through crowded streets, gathering every few minutes to huddle together and to hear again the story of Jesus' passion. This act of devotion makes each participant part of Jesus' last day. It forms our hearts to choose the way of sacrifice, giving, caring. It aids us in putting to death our persistent self-interest and self-centeredness. It disposes our hearts to cruciform choices.

In the early 1900's St. Thomas' Church in New York City was collecting money for a building fund, which would be used to erect a new church on Fifth Avenue. In 1905 a great earthquake nearly destroyed San Francisco. After prayer and consideration the rector of St. Thomas' gave away the entire building fund for relief work in that devastated city. Part of what astonishes me is that most of the members thoroughly approved of the rector's decision. That ex-emplifies a cruciform decision. They started again on the building fund, quickly recouped their donations, and erected what some consider the most beautiful church in the New York.

We baptized people always walk the way of the cross. We always have the ability to make cruciform choices.

In closing, allow me to suggest five paths that may help you in cruciform living. First, get a crucifix. Put it in a place where you can easily see it, and where it will capture your attention. Simply look at it, allow your mind to wrap itself around it, and be quiet before it. I have tried to find meaning in the death of Jesus, but certain aspects of the cross lie beyond the realm of words. We can only access those deeper meanings by empathetic contemplation.

Second, develop an active eucharistic piety. This central act of Christian worship has numerous meanings, but surely remembrance forms one prominent implication. In the scriptural sense remembrance means allowing the past to become part of the present. So, to eat the bread and drink from the cup involves this active remembrance, which is empowered, of course, by the presence of the Risen Lord. In and through this sacrament Christ lives in us and we live in him. By participating faithfully and often in the Eucharist our hearts, minds, and wills are shaped into the form of the cross.

Three, choose to be an agent of the cross in a place of pain. Our world is full of longing and need, and we can become part of Christ's sacrificial caring for the world. In my last parish, we discovered that food was available to the poor every day of the week except Sunday. So, several congregations worked together to provide a hot lunch to all comers on Sunday afternoons. People were eager to serve and gave generously of their time and treasure. They made a cruciform choice and thereby stood with Jesus in a place of need.

Four, acknowledge the pain active in your life. Most of us enjoy the idea that we are capable people who can take care of our own problems, but all of us reach a place where we cannot cope any longer. We may choice to ignore the pain, or we can try to cover it with alcohol or entertainment. But it never really goes away. Because of the cross we can safely open our hearts to

God, knowing that God knows and cares about our problems and struggles. We can chose to cast our burden on Jesus.

Five, take your pain to church. Over the years I have been caught short when people tell me they have ceased attending church because of a divorce, loss of a job, or some other problem. In times like that, sacrament, scripture, and prayer are exactly what we need. I find that as I kneel before the altar as part of the receiving communion that I can pass my problems to Jesus as he is giving himself to me in the sacrament.

Many years ago a member of the church appeared late one afternoon at my office. I had seen his name on the church roll, but had not noted his attendance at worship. He was beside himself with anguish. As he wept he told me that his wife that afternoon had informed him that she now had a job and was leaving him that very day. He had not had any sign that she was unhappy. We meet a number of times as he worked his way through grief and shock. He finally insisted that I take a gift from him. With that token of his thanks I purchased a wooden crucifix which all these years later continues to hang over my desk. When I look at it I sometimes think of that man and wonder what has happened to him. But even more it sparks a deep gratitude in me that I was able to offer a message of comfort and hope to him, all because our Lord shares in our deepest distress and makes it part of his own heart.

Discussion questions:

First, by means of the cross God embraced the pain of the world. Does that give you comfort and hope? If so, why?

Second, sacrifice has been a key concept in this chapter. How would you define that term in your own words? Where in your life are you called to sacrifice? What does it cost you to make that sacrifice?

Third, he cross demonstrates how valuable we are to God. In light of that, how does that change your view of yourself?

Fourth, the cross causes us to view the pain of life in a new way. How would you describe that? What does it look like in your own life?

Next, how would you respond to someone who says that the pain of the world is evidence that God has absented God's self from the world?

Sixth, how would explain to a friend that the cross breaks the usual cycle of revenge and violence?

Seventh, how does the cross call the church to stewardship of the earth?

And last, what are some of the cruciform choices God is presenting to you and your church?

Chapter 7

Death's Dominion Destroyed

Now we move to consider the biblical material concerning the resurrection of Jesus. In doing so we enter the grandest and most mysterious of the four major events in Christ's life. All the elements of the first three episodes are pulled together in a stunning climax to the Jesus story.

One of my favorite composers is the nineteenth century Austrian Anton Bruckner. In the last moments of his eighth symphony he achieves a staggering musical feat. In those closing measures he states all the major themes of the symphony simultaneously. It is calculated to bowl over listeners both emotionally and intellectually. This accomplishment accounts for part of the reason that some have begun to refer to this composition as "*the* symphony."

In a similar way the resurrection fulfills all that has gone before in Jesus' story. For this reason Paul can write that if the resurrection did not happen then our faith is futile. (I Cor 15:14) The resurrection makes Jesus' life *the* story, the grandest chapter of human history.

In order to explore some of the richness of the resurrection we will look at four representative episodes from the gospel of John. They will serve as four photos that allow us to engage in the details of this fourth chapter in Jesus' life, thereby permitting us to do some deep exploration of the Easter event. The New Testament, however, contains many other accounts of the resurrection and many more texts that explicate its meaning. I hope this approach will allow you to be exposed to enough of the Easter event for you to be able to ponder the meaning of that event for yourself and for the church. If you wish to study the resurrection stories in depth and with a scholarly approach I recommend Christopher Bryan's *The Resurrection of the Messiah* or N.T. Wright's *The Resurrection of the Son of God.*

Before we proceed with our study, we need to be clear about what we mean by Jesus' resurrection. I help us get underway we turn to likely the oldest report of that event, the one written by Paul in about 54 AD

> For I handed on to you as of first importance what I in turn had received: that Christ died for our sins in accordance with the scriptures, and that he was buried, and that he was raised on the third day in accordance with the scriptures, and that he appeared to Cephas, then to the twelve. Then he appeared to more than five hundred brothers and sisters at one time, most of whom are still alive, though some have died. Then he appeared to James, then to all the apostles. Last of all, as to one untimely born, he appeared also to me. (1 Cor 15:3–8)

First, the terms Paul uses for "handed on . . . received" are technical terms used in rabbinic circles for material that has been carefully memorized. Our practice of publicly reciting poetry suggests what Paul is saying.

Then note that a number of witnesses are listed with the idea that the reader could seek out some of these persons for further questioning. This precludes any thought of the resurrection appearances as mass hypnosis or the like. The passage, moreover, suggests that Jesus was able to come and go in a way not limited by time and space; this traditionally is called "the glorified body" of Christ. Finally, as Paul notes the resurrection represents a matter of highest importance and priority for all people.

Other accounts help fill out our understanding. In Matthew's gospel we are told that Roman soldiers were posted to assure that Jesus' body was not stolen (Matt 27:62–68). In Luke's version the Risen Christ appears to the disciples and invites them both to observe his punctured hands and feet and to touch him (Luke 24:39).

These factors demonstrate that the Jesus who died on the cross is the same Jesus of Easter, and that the one they knew to be cold stone dead was raised again to life. Furthermore, the touching of his body shows that this is not a ghost or some other paranormal event.

Finally, the gospel accounts are both concise and unemotional. They have the ring of truth about them, and the evangelists clearly depict the events as actual fact. Nothing about them suggests that the resurrection was simply an interior experience of the disciples, that Jesus was raised in their minds and imagination rather than in concrete reality.

Given this background we can now attempt a definition. On the third day after his death, Jesus was raised by the power of God in such a way that he lives beyond the dominion of death, and continues to live and to be available to all persons in all places at all times. This was not a ghost, mistaken identity, resuscitation, recovery from a coma, mass hysteria, a case of a stolen body, or a mere mental perception. All of these alternative explanations are ruled out by the details of the story. The only interpretation that does justice to the biblical texts and that explains both the radical change in the disciples and the rise of the church is resurrection by the power of God. That will stand as our definition of the resurrection of Jesus Christ.

With that in mind we now stand ready to grapple with four representative stories about Jesus' resurrection. We can think of them as acts in an unfolding drama. We find them in John chapter twenty.

Act one is found in John 20:1–10. Here we find Mary Magdalene, one of Jesus' most devoted disciples, making her way in the pre-dawn darkness to the tomb of Jesus. Earlier we have been told that Mary Magdalene had been a witness to the death of Jesus and presumably to his burial. Jewish custom at that time deposited dead bodies in cave-like chambers carved out of rock, the entrance to which was covered with a large rock similar to a mill stone. We are not told why she makes such a sad, lonely trip in the dark. When she arrives she finds that stone rolled away. This prompts her to run to Peter and "the other disciple" to tell them that someone has stolen the body and that she does not know where it is. A pur-loined body, we have to admit, is the simplest and most believable explanation for an empty tomb.

As a side note, "the other disciple", sometimes also called "the disciples whom Jesus loved," is the source of this gospel. At the end of the gospel, we read, "This is the disciple who is testifying to these things, and has written them, and we know that his testimo-ny is true." (John 21:24) Scholars have several explanations about the development of this gospel, but we can reliably say that the foundation of it consists of the witness of this unnamed follower of Jesus. The tradition of the church has been to call him John.

To continue, Peter and the other disciple run to the tomb. The disciple reaches it first, bows down to look in and sees only the linen burial cloths. Peter arrives and enters the tomb, and he too sees the linen clothes neatly lying there. We are told that the other disciple believes in the resurrection on the basis of what he saw in the tomb, namely, burial items but no body. Both then return home.

We are now able to draw some conclusions about the events of act one. The first step in thinking about the resurrection con-cerns the empty tomb. If there was a resurrection the tomb must necessarily be empty, but this fact alone is subject to several alter-native explanations. The "other disciple," however, comes to some level of belief in the resurrection on the evidence of the empty tomb. The only suggestion that something other than grave rob-bing had taken place is that the linen wrappings were in the tomb. If the body had been taken it would likely have been carried off still enclosed in the burial cloths.

The conclusion of this act finds the two disciples simply returning home. If they had had a fuller understanding of resur-rection one would have expected rejoicing and the need to share and talk about this mystery. Recently my wife and I got caught in a crowd of people exiting a major league basketball game. We instantly knew that the home team had lost, because the fans were simply returning home, no excitement, no recapping the game, no wonder at the skills of the players. They just went home. And that is what Peter and the other disciple did.

In act two, Mary Magdalene returns to center stage. This is recorded in John 20:11–18. While the two disciples return home, Mary stays at the tomb weeping. She now bends down to look into the tomb and sees there two angels. They ask why she is in tears, and she repeats her understanding that the body of Jesus has been taken and she does not know where it is. She does not appear to react to the presence of the angels as one might expect. When she turns she sees the Risen Lord, but does not recognize him. He, too, asks why she is weeping. She assumes that Jesus is the gardener, and repeats still again her idea about the body being stolen. At this point Jesus simply speaks her name, she realizes who it is, and exclaims "Rabbouni," which means "dear teacher." Next, she seems to grab hold of Jesus, and he tells her not to hold him. He says that he is on his way back to the Father, almost as if he had made a small detour in order to encounter her. Then Jesus commissions her to carry a message to the disciples: "I am ascending to my Father and your Father, to my God and your God." (vs 17) She returns to the disciples with her stunning announcement: "I have seen the Lord." (vs 18)

We can now debrief this act. This is the first resurrection appearance. Previously we have dealt only with an empty tomb, but here the Risen Jesus meets Mary Magdalene. Part of what is remarkable is that in Jesus' time the testimony of a woman had no legal standing, but here the evangelist records what would have been puzzling to first century readers, that a woman was the first witness and the first to proclaim the resurrection.

Twice Mary Magdalen is asked why she is weeping. Surely this signifies the compassion and care of those who meet her. They see and acknowledge her grief. But more than that, both the angels and Jesus are asking Mary to come to a new level of awareness. The question seems to imply that probing the deep parts of her grief can lead her beyond mere sorrow. Perhaps she would have found that her devotion would not be in vain. Beneath the tears may have lain an intuition that the death of Jesus was not the end of his story.

Jesus speaks Mary's name, and on the basis of that alone she recognizes him. Previously in chapter ten Jesus says that he is the good shepherd, and that his sheep would recognize his voice (John 10:3).

One of the breakthrough moments in this act arrives when Jesus proclaims that his God and Father is also the God and Father of his disciples. In the past, he has spoken of them as disciples and even as friends, but now they are allowed to enter into the intimate relationship that Jesus has with the Father. The disciples now participate in the love that unifies Jesus and his Father. The resurrection has opened the door to a new depth of connectedness between Jesus and the disciples.

The evangelist highlights the fact that Jesus was buried and raised in a garden and that Jesus was mistakenly perceived as a gardener. This is no casual detail. The biblical story begins in the garden of Eden, where the perfection of life is marred by the disobedience of the man and the woman. The Bible ends with a vision of the restored Jerusalem in which grows a garden, where the tree of life produces fruit for the healing of the nations. The resurrection comprises the pivot point between the opening and ending of scripture. In the person of Jesus and his resurrection the tragedy of Eden is reversed and the process of the restoration of all creation is begun.

Finally, note the testimony of Mary Magdalene to the disciples: "I have seen the Lord." (v.18) She has, of course, seen the Risen One with her eyes, but she also has had an important insight. Jesus of Nazareth is now Jesus the risen Lord. Sight and insight have merged, resulting in the first statement indicating an understanding of what had occurred that day in the garden.

Act three advances the drama of the Easter story. This can be found in John 20:19–24. The action takes place in a locked room on Easter evening, and we discover the disciples there huddled in fear. Apparently they have not digested the testimony of Mary Magdalene, because they are in hiding, shrinking before the possibility that the authorities might arrest and execute them. Suddenly, Jesus simply is there among them. He gives his disciples the gift of peace, and then shows them his punctured hands and side. This act implies that the person who died on the cross is now present;

this is not a ghost or a case of mistaken identity. Through this narrative we witness the amazing phenomenon that the Risen Jesus is physically present, yet in such a way that locked doors and solid walls do not hinder him.

Now the atmosphere changes. The disciples rejoice when they recognize the Lord. What follows is Jesus gracing his disciples with three gifts. First is peace. Remember that in the Bible this is not simply the absence of conflict, but represents a quality of life in the presence of God. Peace consists of God providing all that one needs to be the person God intends that person to be. Peace consists of knowing that God is present and provident.

Next, Jesus says, "As the Father has sent me, so I send you." (vs 20) Now the disciples will participate in the mission of God inaugurated by Jesus. It is through the disciples that the ministry of Jesus will continue. They will be the voice, hands, and feet of the Risen One.

Finally, Jesus gifts them both with the presence and the authority of the Holy Spirit. Here Jesus breathes on them in a way that recalls the second chapter of Genesis where God breathes life into the creature God has made from the dust of the ground. And the authority Jesus gives is significant. He states, "If you forgive the sins of any, they are forgiven them; if you retain the sins of any, they are retained." (vs 23) They have been made authorized agents of the grace of God; it is through them that reconciliation will be mediated.

Before we proceed to the last act please note a significant shift in this act. There is a four step movement from fear to recognition to rejoicing to ministry. This is a playing out of the paschal mystery. When and wherever the Risen Christ is present and active the result will be this pattern of the paschal mystery. Fear will be turned into joy, despair into hope, lethargy into energy. The paschal mystery represents the paradigm of the lives of the baptized.

You can find act four in John 20:24–29. One of the disciples, Thomas, had been absent when the events of act three took place. The others took up the now-familiar phrase: "we have seen the Lord." (vs 25) But Thomas makes an emphatic reply: unless I see the punctures and put my finger in the marks in his hands and side, I will not ever believe.

On the following Sunday the disciples were again gathered, but this time Thomas was present. The doors were again shut, but that did not stop the Risen Jesus entering and being with the group. Once more, Jesus greets them with "Peace be with you," and then he turns his attention to Thomas. Jesus commands his disciples to touch his wounded hands and side, and then he adds, "Do not doubt but believe." (vs 27) To this Thomas announces the clearest and highest declaration of faith in this gospel: "My Lord and my God!" (vs 28)

At the conclusion of this act, it is as if Jesus turns and addresses the readers: "Blessed are those who have not seen and yet have come to believe." (vs 29) Thomas's faith appears to be based on sight and touch, but that option is not open to the readers. But that fact need not stand as a barrier to faith. Verses thirty and thirty one state that faith in the Risen Christ can be generated by encountering him in the written word of this gospel.

As we step back and take an analytical look at act four, we note that doubt forms a part of the resurrection account. And this represents a refreshingly honest assessment of our response to the declaration that Jesus has been raised from the dead by the power of God. We cannot deny that resurrection taxes our credulity. Our sense is that everything passes away, that the dead stay dead, and that death speaks the last word on life. And then we are encountered by the stunning proclamation of Jesus' resurrection, which lays before us an event utterly unique and beyond our ability to explain. In reading these gospel stories today, Jesus simply appears in our consciousness and offers peace, but disbelief could, nevertheless, be our primary and only response. Yet both the stories and the experience of two millennia of Christians stand. We can go so far as to say that doubt is necessarily an element of faith, and without it faith does not exist. The opposite of faith, so these resurrection stories seem to suggest, is indifference, not doubt.

Another striking element consists of Jesus' command to believe. My sense is that he is challenging Thomas to move on, to step out, to be open to God-given possibilities, and to test those possibilities. Recall the Danish philosopher Soren Kierkegaard, who coined the phrase "the leap of faith." Jesus called Thomas to step out of the doubt mode and into mode of potentiality. When Thomas did he found that the resurrection was more than a possibility.

We today do not have access to the experience of Thomas. We cannot touch Jesus' hands and side. But we do have entry into faith by means of the story. Much of what we hold to be true comes to us via the witness of others whom we trust. For example, I was intrigued to hear in a documentary that no artifacts of the Battle of Hastings have ever been found, but we do have the recorded stories of those who were there, and thereby we trust that that event did occur. In a similar way Jesus promises blessing to those who can come to faith by means of the gospel story.

The artist Caravaggio painted "The Incredulity of Thomas" in 1601–02. The background of this vivid and emotional work is simply black. On the left stands the Risen Lord wrapped in white clothes, looking fit and young. The light seems both to shine on and come from Jesus.

Standing on the right is Thomas, dressed in torn clothes and looking weary. To me Thomas eyes seem to be those of a blind man. Over Thomas's shoulder stand two disciples, slightly bent in an attempt to see what is transpiring between Jesus and Thomas. I believe that we are to understand them as Peter and the beloved disciple. Jesus has grabbed Thomas's arm and pulled it toward him, and Thomas is in the act of putting his index finger into the wound in Jesus's side. Indeed, Thomas has inserted his finger up to the second joint into the wound.

For me it is a painting from which I can barely turn away. It captures that exact moment when Jesus is responding to Thomas's doubt. Jesus' response is to push Thomas's human finger into his risen body. These four wondrous resurrection stories allow to push our human minds into the realm of divine life, love, and victory. We can be there with the Risen One.

Discussion questions:

First, as you consider the characters in the johannine account of Easter, which one do you most identify with?

Second, John raises issues about faith. In light of our study how would you define faith?

Third, the resurrection turns the world of the disciples upside-down. Has the resurrection changed your life? Are you able to give examples?

Fourth, can you identify the movements of the paschal mystery in your life and in the life of your church?

Chapter 8

Words of Life

MANY ANGLICAN CHURCHES BUILT in the eighteenth century in both England and the United States had a unique feature. Large wooden tablets have been placed on the wall behind the altar. One had written on it, usually in gold letter, the Lord's Prayer, another the Creed, and the third the Ten Commandments. These tablets represented on attempt to instill knowledge and piety in the worshippers.

The Creed embodies the basics of the Christian faith by stating foundational beliefs about the Father, the Son, and the Holy Spirit. The Lord's Prayer stands as the example of how to pray in light of the statements of the Creed. And the Ten Commandments instruct readers about how to live if one believes the Creed and prays the Lord's Prayer.

The Decalogue, the ten words, is a common alternative title for the Ten Commandments. The ancient commandments given to Moses were likely very concise, so much so that they could properly be called the ten words. I suggest that term can also be used to describe how a person should and can live well in light of the God revealed in Jesus Christ. A resurrectional Decalogue, therefore, can be seen as words about how we can shape our lives in light of Easter.

The issue addressed in this chapter is how a baptized believer can live life in light of the glorious resurrection of Jesus Christ from the dead. How can we be Easter people? How can we become people who have stepped out of the darkness of the tomb and into the light of the Risen Lord? How can we keep the resurrection before us in a manner similar to the wooden tablets in those eighteenth century churches?

I have organized this chapter in terms of ten short statements, which I believe represent implications of the resurrection. The ten statements lay out how a person can live well, knowing that he or she has been united to Christ via baptism. I do not see these as restrictive or mandatory commandments. But I do see them simply as words of life stated in a concise manner. They function as a resurrectional Decalogue.

As a young man George Washington developed a list of statements entitled *Rules of Civility and Decent Behavior.* He wrote a hundred and ten succinct sentences, which describe the kind of man he wanted to be. In a similar way my hope is that my ten words will help you state what kind of resurrection people we endeavor to be.

First, finish off fear. Years ago I went to the airport with my parents so that my father could catch a plane for a business assignment. As the plane was lifting off from the runway, my mother said, "I just hate it when he flies." I responded with an unhelpful statement: "Flying is six times safer than riding in a car." Her anxiety was not a matter of safety or reason. She said, "Yes, but in a car you can control what happens." And there it is! Fear grows out of the soil of the need for control.

That desire to manage and direct forms a deep and basic part of who we are. We want to supervise so that we can avoid death and the deathly experiences that constitute part of the life of every human being. If we can just control the steering wheel we hope we can avoid painful episodes that choke the life out of us.

Looming behind all of this stands the shadow of death, our old enemy. Who of us does not have anxiety about dying? And it is not just a matter of physical death when our heart ceases to function, but we also dread the little deaths that make up our daily existence. Think of failure, pain, loneliness, guilt, lack of purpose, poverty as examples of little deaths. They make us die a little on the inside, in our imagination and heart and will. Thus we spent a good portion of our energy and time seeking ways to control events to avoid the shadow of death.

And it happens in the church, too. I encounter something close to panic in some congregations because of declining attendance and giving, all of which is exacerbated by no apparent way to manage the decline or prevent institutional death. "If we don't do something we will die" is a refrain I hear too often. But no clear answer presents itself in response to that painful and fearful statement.

Over forty years ago I found myself in small room at a church retreat center. I was appearing before the committee that had a major say in determining whether I was to be ordained or not. I had been through four years of college and three years of seminary, and I had endured a week of ordination exams and even more time writing an extensive theological paper. But in that room the moment of truth had arrived. I experienced something that day that has happened only once or twice in my life. In the midst of the questions and answers I noticed that I had developed shooting pains in both wrists. Out of fright my blood vessels had constricted so much that throbbing cramps set in. That disturbing sign told me that I was facing the possible death of a dream and life-plan. And I could not control the situation.

In summary, we have plotted the connection between fear and the desire to control our lives in the face of the threat of dying. These fears, moreover, form cracks in the very foundation of our lives. That is, fear is not small matter that we should simply ignore. Rather, it signifies a deep disturbance at the very center of our being.

Some years back I had gone to my physician about a sore throat, and in the process of the exam he measured my blood pressure. Both he and I were surprised to find that I had a high pressure reading. The years that followed saw various techniques and strategies to control this silent and dangerous condition. I now take a medicine that relaxes my whole circulatory system. My heart rate has slowed and the pressure readings are well within normal range. With the help of that medicine life blood flows freely throughout my body.

Resurrection can function in a similar way. It serves as an injection of life in place of fear, and it causes our entire emotional apparatus to relax. The fact of the resurrection and our relying on it changes radically our approach to life, including fear and anxiety. Resurrection destroys fear and explodes anxiety. Resurrection forms a place of refuge and safety.

Here is how it works. First, recall our discussion of the paschal mystery in the last chapter. This refers to the pattern of Jesus' story, a movement from death to new life. Consider that as the consistent pattern by which God works. When God is present, God's action will take whatever is deathly and make something good and life-giving from it. This is not being optimist or finding the silver lining in every cloud; those represent mere wishes that have no particular foundation. Resurrection, however, is based on what God did for Jesus. Resurrection and the paschal mystery are not wishes and desires, but rather are facts about the manner in which God chooses to deal with humanity.

We also need to recall the place of baptism in the paschal mystery. When a person is baptized God in fact acts on that person and changes his or her basic identity. God unites the baptismal candidate with the death and resurrection of Christ. That person's life is folded into the story of Jesus. The identity of that person is rooted in Jesus and the shape of their lives will be defined by the paschal mystery. In baptism God promises to be present with us, always making life of death.

I hasten to add that the paschal mystery is not the promise of a life with no deathly events in it. It is not a free pass from the pains and perplexities of existence. But it does establish that nothing we do is done in vain, that our lives do have purpose and meaning, and that whatever we offer of ourselves to God will somehow benefit God's mission of new life for the whole creation.

Think of the years of turmoil, threat, and struggle that Desmond Tutu endured in his fight for justice in South Africa. God took all of that pain and reshaped it to serve as part of the energy that transformed his country.

Next, think about the role of trust in the baptismal promise. The assurance of resurrection will not come to fruition if we do not give it a chance. We must be willing to put it to the test, to proceed as if it really is true, and make a leap of faith into the future. For instance, if I did not trust that a bridge could support me as I crossed over it I would never venture onto that bridge. But I could make my journey if I trusted that the bridge could do what it was designed to do. Resurrection asks us to trust that God will do for us what he did for Jesus.

As we learn to trust in the presence of resurrection power in our lives, the Eucharist is the sacramental form of the resurrection. We bring the altar the problems and pains of our life and we make them part of what we offer to Christ. In turn, the Risen Christ gives us his presence in and under the bread and the wine of the sacrament. The Eucharist is possible, after all, only because Jesus is risen and graciously chooses to feed us with his presence, his body and blood.

Regular participation in the Eucharist, therefore, shapes our hearts to trust in the redeeming presence of God in our lives.

All of this applies to the church, too. Fear in congregational and diocesan life paralyzes any sense that we are both called to carry on the mission of Christ and that he will empower it with his presence. Churches need to probe the sources of fear, an act that in itself requires trust that God can make something good from the unsavory parts of congregational life. Fear in this setting denotes a threat to the future of the church and the empowerment of its members. The Risen Lord stands as the head of the church, and that means we have an infinite source of resurrection power in the life of our congregations.

I live near Yellowstone Park. Our area news media have been reporting a recent spate of disasters there. Several people have wandered off the boardwalk and fallen into hots springs. In one such case the heat killed and the man and the acidic content of the water apparently dissolved his body. Other come dangerously close to bison in search of an exciting snapshot. One person put a bison calf in the tack of his SUV because he thought the animal looked cold.

These are situations that call for a sensible dose of fear. Fright does, in fact, remind us that it is not an end in itself, but that we have alternative ways of acting. But the powerful fears that hinder and paralyze us point us to the God and the power of the resurrection. Fear need not be a defining factor in our lives.

When I sit in my cathedra several features in the church always draw my attention. One of those is a shield mounted on the rood beam, the large timber support that stretches across the width of the front of the church. I am one of the few who sees it, because it is mounted on the back of the beam. It contain four letter: NIKE. In Greek, this spells victory. That represents the last word about life in the resurrection. Christ was victorious. That is the very word I need to hear. How about you?

Second, have courage. Standing in front of the Houses of Parliament in London is a monumental statue of King Richard I. He has his huge sword held high above him, his war horse is stomping the ground, and his face glows with confidence and self-assurance. Here stands a portrayal of a ruler ready for action. His nickname was Richard Coeur de Lion, Richard Lionheart. To his subjects he represented the epitome of courage and valor.

The root of the word "courage" is heart. The place inside ourselves where emotions, thoughts, will, and imagination come together we call our heart. Courage, then, involves the confidence and hope that grows out of the center of our being.

But having courage is harder than practicing it. We all know that we face genuine danger every day. We could be involved in a fatal car accident. We could be struck down by a heart attack or stroke. We could be a victim of random violence. It is a scary world at there. Simply to say that we plan to be courageous may not equip us for genuine courage in action.

The question becomes: can we find a way to see beyond and around possible danger, disaster, and even death. Some years back my wife and I saw a superb production of *Hamlet* by the Royal

Shakespeare Company. The play concludes with every major character lying dead on the stage. Both my wife and I left limp and drained after several hours of a story about revenge, fear, and murder. Part of our response was based on the fact that bloodshed and retribution had taken charge of our hearts. The play pushes the disasters of life so firmly in the face that death was all we could see. Any courage had been drained out of us.

But the end of the biblical story takes a completely different turn. The book of Revelation was written to encourage Christians who were facing persecution from the Roman Empire. Some of them had already died for their faith, and the rest were apparently fearful and discouraged by persecution and ostracism. At the end of the book the writer lays out a glorious vision. The new Jerusalem descends from heaven. God is fully present, death is destroyed, and all pain is wiped away. Life and healing prevail. The write possessed a vision, a revelation, that allowed the readers to see through and around the darkness of persecution, fear, and martyrdom.

That wondrous vision grows directly out of the resurrection. If God can conquer death, then God can deal with any contingency that might befall God's people, even the persecutions and injustice of the seemingly all-powerful empire of Rome. The end of the story of the church is victory, the triumph of God, life, and love.

The resurrection of Jesus Christ generates and empowers courage. The church can say that we are able see our way through any disaster, because we are convinced that God can bring life and love out of the worst that can happen to us.

I live in Montana, a state that offers many recreational opportunities. A river float is a favorite. People put a large inner tube in a river, settle themselves inside it, and then let the flow of the river take them for a ride. When I see people doing this I notice the expression of peace on their faces. Christians should remember that we are always afloat in baptismal waters. As noted often before baptism is God's promise to us individually and to the church that our future is resurrection, filled with life and hope. Does that not produce courage in you?

I was sitting in a retreat house in London some years back when Terry Waite walked in. At 6 feet 10 inches he was hard to ignore. He had arrived to speak to a group of young people. From 1987–1991 he was held hostage by a group of Islamic fundamentalists in Lebanon. He had gone there as a special envoy of Robert Runcie, then the Archbishop of Canterbury. His assignment had been to negotiate the release for four hostages, but instead he become one himself.

After his release Waite was often questioned about what had sustained him during those years in prison, often in isolation. He replied that the words of the Book of Common Prayer, which he had grown up with and knew by heart, had been crucial to his survival. He gave as an example using this collect: "Lighten our darkness, we beseech thee, O Lord; and by thy great mercy defend us from all perils and dangers of this night." This prayer grows out of a keen and deep awareness of the reality of the resurrection. The Risen One is present and is able to defend and protect the baptized. This simple collect, found in most of the prayer books in the Anglican Communion, engenders courage and hope. Waite could see around and through the darkness. Courage grows in the garden of the resurrection.

Third, pursue God's plan. God always has a mind-boggling strategy, and God's largest and boldest proposal is the reconciliation of the whole world to God's own self. The author of Ephesians states God's mission eloquently: "With all wisdom and insight [God] has made known to us the mystery of his will, according to his good pleasure that he set forth in Christ, as a plan for the fullness of time, to gather up all things in him, things in heaven and things on earth." (Eph 1.8–9) Note that Christ reveals and executes the divine mission, which consists of bringing into God's embrace all the cosmos. We understand, then, the importance of considering the four major episodes in Jesus' life, and the manner in which they set into motion the mission this grand plan of salvation.

By virtue of our baptism and faith we are called into the great plan of God. In the water of baptism God looks at us and says, "I want you. I have important work for you. I recruit you for my plan of salvation of the whole universe." Can you imagine a grander purpose in life? Can you think of anything greater in which a person can invest him or herself?

When I chat with young people I often ask what they want to do with their future. "I'm not sure" is the most common reply. And the facial expression that accompanies it usually is fear.

Finding the direction of one's life is not an unimportant undertaking. Having a sense of purpose, believing that our life has significance and value, forms one of the most basic needs for human beings. Our culture asks to settle for a snack food answer to the issue of purpose. Make money, have a comfortable home, enjoy nice vacations. Like potato chips these things may taste good, but offer little to sustain life. Self-interest and seeking one's own benefit form the basis of these goals. They go nowhere and lead to nothing significant.

The resurrection radically raises the standards. We are asked to give ourselves to Christ, knowing that nothing we offer is in vain, but will lead to new creation. The resurrection declares that we are on the side of God's life and love, and, in fact, are agents of them. The resurrection assists us to perceive that life and love embody the power to change the universe.

Each of us is born with unique characteristics, talents, and interests. We can call these gifts of creation. But we also receive gifts in baptism, abilities that can be harnessed by the Risen Christ. I, for instance, have always had an interest in books, writing, and communication. When I sensed that I might be called to the priesthood I was afraid that I might lack the talent to do that work, particularly in preaching. Boring, lifeless preaching is something to be feared by all! The work of college and seminary, however, showed that I had gifts that could be developed so that I might become an effective preacher. Gifts of creation and gifts of baptism came together, and allow me to take my part in God's mission.

The paschal mystery serves as a warranty on the time, talent, and energy we offer to the Risen One. Remember that God can take what we give and make something good and life-giving from it. For example, I have at times preached sermons that I thought missed the target, but then someone would say, "Thank you for that sermon. It blessed me." Those sorts of comments have always come to me as a surprise, and signify paschal mystery at work.

I often drive roads that parallel the main line of the BNSF railroad. Someone is always at work, repairing track, cutting grass, driving locomotives, and even directing the flow of train traffic from the central office in far-away Fort Worth. We, all of us, are called to work on God's railroad, using what skills we have to God's grant purpose. None of us has all that is needed, but by working together God can further God's mission.

Most of the time the ministry we called to do is common and ordinary. But that is part of the wonder of being a person who pursues God's plan; even the small things count. Honest work, being a consistently compassionate presence, giving generously to godly causes, setting an example of kindness and patience, saying a good word about the church, sharing a bit of your God story, being a reflective spouse and parent, offering all you do to the glory of God—these embody the purposes of God and exemplify God's will.

Two factors denote our active participation in God's mission. First, it is not self-serving, but Christ-serving. The essence of what separates us from God is our assumption that life is about us. For instance, what is it that you think about when you are not thinking about anything else? Is it not yourself? And is it not yourself seen in the best possible light? That persistent tendency is what the church means by original sin. That constant self-centeredness constitutes the place from which all other sins arise. And we all know that dealing with this tendency is life-long work. We can, however, understand that the way that leads to life for ourselves and others focuses on the incarnate, baptized, crucified, and risen Christ. And we can commit ourselves to keeping our eyes on that prize.

The second factor is that we freely give our talents, skills, and interests understanding that Christ will use them to work the wonders of the paschal mystery in the world. This flows naturally from our love for Jesus, who loved us and gave himself for us. For example, as I write this my wife and I are celebrating our wedding anniversary. I enjoy doing things for her, and when she asks for help I am usually eager to do that. I certainly do not expect a pay check for doing dishes and taking out the garbage. I do what I do for her out of love. Can we do anything else in regard to our love of Jesus?

The first of the great monastic groups in the western church is the Order of St. Benedict. The motto of the order is "Ora et Labora." Pray and work. Is that not the way we can pursue God's purpose?

Four, become a church renewer. I recently made an official visitation to one of my churches. As soon as I walked through the door I knew a new day, an Easter day, had dawned there. I heard the buzz of people talking, I could see others getting ready for the various events of the weekend, and I had a lively discussion with the rector and vestry about what they perceived as resurrection happening among them. It made my heart sing, because I believe that a primary agent of God's mission is the local congregation.

In a time when churches are often overlooked and ignored, remember that one of the first things the Risen Lord did was found the church. We have previously studied the episode in John chapter twenty where the Risen Lord appears to his fearful disciples on the evening of the first Easter. He gives them the gifts of peace, the presence of the Spirit, and then he passes to them his ministry. He declares, "Receive the Holy Spirit. If you forgive the sins of any, they are forgiven them; if you retain the sins of any, they are retained." (John 20:22–23) The church has been fully equipped to carry out its noble and essential work. Please note this carefully: Christ himself formed and continues to guide his church.

Add to the divine origin of the church the fact that we cannot be Christians alone. The Risen Lord works through other people, and that means through the church. Someone might reply that the church is full of hypocrites and sinners. This is most certainly true, but that comment could be made about almost any group. One of the truths of life together as church can be that what we most need to hear often comes from the people who annoy and hurt us. I have been called to a higher quality of work, for example, by the criticism of others, even though I do not enjoy what they had to say. Even the grumblers and grouches have their role to play.

We read the Bible best together, we worship best together, we carry out ministry best together. If we try to go it alone, discouragement easily sets in. Or we develop idiosyncratic readings of scripture. Or our worship becomes comforting to ourselves rather than glorifying God. We cannot baptize ourselves. The Eucharist cannot be celebrated with only one person. Everything about the church suggests that it must be a community.

One of the most interesting developments in the early church was the phenomenon of men and women going into the deserts of Egypt and Israel to become hermits. When the church became a legal religion in the fourth century, some serious Christians saw it compromising with the culture and becoming lukewarm. They felt impelled to be alone in order to pray and be closer to Christ, unencumbered by the influences of a secular culture and a weakened church. But even these people made their way to church on Sunday to take part together in the Eucharist. At the burning heart of their commitment was the community of Christ gathered to hear his word and receive his body and blood.

People can dismiss the church fairly easily. Some see it as relevant only for those who are religiously inclined, and others view it as just another organization in the community. Probably the least helpful opinion states that the church is a collection of hypocrites or do-gooders. The New Testament itself, however, lays before us a description of the church that I, at least, find energizing and inspiring. In both Romans and 1 Corinthians Paul describes the church as the body of Christ. He does not say that it is like the body of Christ; he is not speaking in similes.

Rather, in a mystical yet authentic way the church is, in fact, the body of Christ. I suspect that this view arose from Paul's conversion experience. You remember that Paul was going to Damascus to arrest Christians, and along the way he is encountered by the Risen Christ in the form of light and a voice. So shocking is this that Paul falls to the ground, and the voice of Christ then says, "Why do you persecute me?(Acts 9:4) Clearly to persecute the Risen One was equal to persecuting the church, and vice-versa. Here a powerful and significant theology of church established itself. In view of the resurrection, we can understand the church as the body of the Risen Lord. The baptized become the eyes and ears, hands and feet of the Lord. The church becomes the agency through which Jesus is present and carries out his reconciling mission. That view of the church as the body of Christ makes it difficult to dismiss the church.

I once taught a junior high Bible class. To help the students understand this concept, I took a long piece of shelf paper and laid it on the floor. I asked the tallest person in the class to lie down, and another student traced his outline on the paper. Then we had a discussion. I asked who thought that they could be good listeners for Jesus. Three raised their hands, so we drew three ears on the outlined body. How can serve others? Four hands were added to the arms. And so we continued. By the end of the exercise we had a very peculiar body, but they had begun to digest the fact that they were, indeed, part of the body of Christ.

If we are going to think of the church in resurrectional terms as we make our spiritual journey through life, we should understand that the church is called to be the community that lives in an alternate reality. We are part of the reign of God, we have stepped out of the tomb and into the light of Easter, and we are citizens of heaven. Again the New Testament book of Acts captures this in its description of the life of the first generation of Christians. We are told that they sold their goods and distributed the proceeds to those in need, and they held all things in common. They spend much time in prayer and participated in the Eucharist in their homes. They were glad, generous worshippers whom everyone held in high regard. (Acts 2:44–47) Clearly they ordered their lives in a remarkably unique way based on their understanding of the implications of resurrection.

To state it another way, being a decent, law-abiding person is not the same as being a Christian. Think about this set of contrasts. The church is about giving, and our society is about consuming. Christians serve and the society functions out of self-interest. Christians seek to worship God and the society seeks entertainment. Christians, then, live with a set of ideals and values that distinguish them from others.

For me an acid test is the purpose of fund-raisers in churches. Is the point to raise money to pay the bills, or is it to help fund an outreach ministry or an organization that serves people?

It is about self or others? In a world of consumers, we need to be part of the alternate resurrection reality by being givers.

As people touched by the Risen Christ we automatically become part of the body of Christ, the church. We all know that it has many flaws and makes many mistakes. But we can live in the new reality by being a renewer of the church, helping it become what it is designed to be.

I was sitting in a concert hall waiting for the beginning of the performance. Behind me a couple were engaged in a serious conversation, one which I could not help but overhear. At one point the man said, "I don't believe in institutional religion." That so angered me that I considered turning to him and asking, "Do you not believe in institutional medical care or in institutional education?" If we see ourselves as renewers of the Body of Christ, we know that the church is simply too important to ignore or dismiss.

Five, develop self-awareness. Many years ago I was part of a workshop on evangelism. One of the major components consisted of learning to tell our God story. The assignment was to sit with someone and narrate our life story in terms of the presence of the Risen Lord active in our lives. I thought to myself, "This will take about two-and-a-half minutes." I did not believe that I had much to tell. I launched into my life journey, and, to my surprise, was still at it four hours later. One instance of the presence of Christ led me to think of another and then another and then another. That afternoon I discovered that my life was packed with instances of Jesus alive and active in my life journey.

We all need to be adept at the ability to note and identify the presence of the Risen Lord in our lives and in our churches. We tend to think that we are not important enough for Christ to be present with us, but the truth is quite the contrary.

I had a friend who became fascinated with discovering God's presence in our life story.

She was not satisfied with simply talking about it and wanted some sort of record. She took a long stretch of shelf paper and on it drew a time line. Above the line she noted significant events: her birth, the first day in school, college, marriage, and so forth. Below the line she worked at writing the events and ways in which resurrection took place in her story. The last time I saw here time line her chart was eighteen feet long. She had scores and scores of events in which Jesus had been presence working resurrection in her life.

This appears to be a simple process. For most of us, an issue stands in the way. Let me illustrate. One of the churches I served had an active adult forum on Sunday mornings. The usual practice consisted of inviting people both from within and outside the church the make presentations. I had invited a pastoral counselor who served on the staff of an agency supported by churches in the community, including that parish. Several weeks before he was scheduled to appear, two couples in the congregation came to me and asked me to cancel the counselor's visit. They said, "We do not believe it is possible for someone to talk with a person and discover what is happening inside that person." I was stunned because these were highly educated and sophisticated people, who, nevertheless, did not seem to understand one of the basic assumptions of counseling. As we chatted the real issue appeared. It was not so much that they did not believe in therapy as much as they were afraid that it did work. What if someone could talk with them and, in fact, understand something of their inner lives? That was simply too frightening for them to cope with.

What if I were to look deep into myself and find there things that scared me, made me ashamed, questioned my beliefs and actions, or would make me look bad to others? That fact is, of course, that is exactly what we would find. We all carry around secret burdens and sins. If we are going to be self-aware enough for us to discover the presence of Christ in our lives we will also uncover aspects of our stories that we wish to hide. We cannot have one without the other.

Self-awareness, then, requires vulnerability. Can we be honest about who we really are? Can we face the facts of our own identity and history? I believe most people cannot do this unless they know they can survive the process. That is, we all need to know that we will not collapse if we face our darker side. Part of my story is that I was able to undergo this process only because I knew that God would accept me no matter what I discovered. And that was for me a resurrectional moment, a time when Jesus was present assuring me of the power of his deathless love. Our odyssey with the Risen One can only be enriched if we are vulnerable enough to open the deepest and darkest part of ourselves to him and to ourselves.

Six, don't fear failure. A long time ago one of my parishioners was going through a divorce. She had been married for years and had two children who were in college and high school. The marriage had ended at the request of the husband, and had come as a complete shock to her. I called on her at her home. I spend several hours with her, and she spent most of that time in tears. Over and over she repeated, "I feel like such a failure."

Failure drains the life out of us. It short-circuits energy, hope, and joy. In Easter terms, failure drives us back into that dark, cold tomb of death.

And churches suffer from this, too. I have talked with vestries that believe they are facing the demise of their church. "We have tried everything, and nothing seems to work," they tell me. I stand with them as they look into the abyss of failure and the eventual death of their church. Gone are hope, vitality, joy, and the ability to take significant action. Again, the events of Easter have disappeared and they are inside the tomb.

Just at this point we need to look at the new life offered in the resurrection. Jesus had died as a complete failure; everything that could go wrong had gone wrong. But thanks be to God that was not the end of his story. God's power raised Jesus to new life, and Jesus continues today to be present mediating divine deathless love into our lives. This exemplifies the miracle of the paschal mystery. Whenever Christ is present, he can bring life out of death. This enables us to deal with failure in a new way. We can say to ourselves that this is not the end of the story and that Christ has some blessing in store for us.

This, however, is easier said than done. How can we move toward new life in the midst of failure? Certainly our basic focus must be that the Christ Jesus is Lord, and he is that exactly by virtue of his redemptive death and life-giving resurrection. In Christ we see not only God's will for us, but also that Jesus is the means of accomplishing God's will.

To put it another way, Jesus becomes our focus. Jesus is the center of the wheel of life; our lives revolve around him and supported by him. He is the conduit of new life, which we can receive through prayer, scripture, and the Eucharist.

I have a friend in whose house is a wall covered from ceiling to floor with various kinds of crosses. It would be hard to ignore the focus on Jesus. Everywhere you move your eyes in that room his symbol is there. Can our view of life be focused in a similar way?

The failures, furthermore, can be used by Christ. In 2 Corinthians Paul uses the image of a clay pot which contains a great treasure. We might even extend the image and speak of a cracked pot. The treasure is the death and resurrection of Christ. We may be humble, even damaged, pots, but the treasure of the Risen Christ is contained in us and thereby the light of life shine from and through us, even if we are failures. (2 Cor 4:7)

Failure can also be embodied in burn-out. We could also term this compassion fatigue. Both result from caring intensely about someone or something and suffering repeated failure. Often coupled with this is a sense of anger. "I have given and given, and nobody cares and nothing changes." Also related is self-blame. "I have done something wrong—I am not sure what it is—and now everything has fallen apart." These are the refrains in the songs of failure.

When we find ourselves singing these sad songs, we can remember who we are and who Jesus is. We are the baptized, who by a special act of God has been united to Christ in his death and resurrection. That certainly stands as the most important fact about our identity. And we look to Christ, the Risen One, knowing that he can bring life out of death. Being baptized into the Living Lord forms the antidote to failure.

One of my churches was beginning to face a bleak future. They had been in decline, and some in-fighting had done further damage. The power of the resurrection showed itself in an unexpected way. Some new members brought with them from their previous church the idea of a clothes closet. The plan was that members would collect clothing, wash it, and make it available free of charge to people who needed clothes. That idea sparked action, and it brought new life and hope. The last time I visited that congregation five thousand people per month visited the clothes closet, and the church had begun offering food in addition to clothes. It is the paschal mystery in action.

Seven, resurrection breaks barriers. In 2003 my own Episcopal Church entered a time of deep division over the gay issue. The precipitating event was the ordination as bishop of an opening gay man in partnered relationship. Both sides claimed biblical warrant and convincing arguments based on reason. At this point the charges and name calling reached a disturbingly strong and bitter pitch. The liberals claimed that the conservatives did not care about gay persons and were out of touch with the times. The conservatives countered with the charge that the liberals did not care about the Bible and were being unfaithful to the orthodox tradition of the church. After the wrenching 2003 General Convention the energy was sapped out of the church; no one seemed to be able to proceed even on significant matters. The lines were drawn and the guns loaded, but no one had the energy to act.

The early church had a similar issue. The questions was if Gentiles could be Christians without first becoming Jews. Jesus himself was, after all, Jewish, and the Old Testament asserted again and again that non-Jews, the Gentiles, were outside the purview of God's concern.

Both sides had arguments based on scripture, and both viewed the other with suspicion and anger.

In both the above instances fear of the "other" seemed to be involved. He or she is not my race, my gender, my sexual orientation, my people and nation. Behind that fear lies self-protection. If we allow the "other" into the community, we might be tainted, scattered, or even destroyed.

Both examples constitute a form of death for all involved. Energy is short-circuited, fear wins the day, Christ's mission is forgotten. The pain of dying steps to center stage and darkness sets in the hearts of all involved.

The early church faced the Jews versus Gentile problem head on. In Acts Peter is confronted with a dream in which God instructs him to eat all sorts of animals, even those that Jewish people considered unclean. The next day Peter meets a Cornelius, a Gentile who had invited Peter to visit his home as the result of his own dream. Peter gets the point. In Christ not only are all animals declared clean, but all people are deemed acceptable. Peter begins a sermon to Cornelius's household with this: "I truly perceive that God shows no partiality." (Acts 10:34) His sermon concludes with a bold proclamation of Jesus' resurrection.

In Acts chapter fifteen a similar story occurs. Paul tells the elders of the church gathered in Jerusalem about the conversions of many Gentiles. The leader of the Jerusalem church, Jesus' brother James, declares that God was at work among the Gentiles and that the church should accept them. By hindsight this became one of the most important events in church history.

Both of these significant events are resurrectional. Christ had broken decisively the barrier of death, and the Risen Christ was at work even among the Gentiles. For the Risen One, human barriers have ceased to exist, and now the Christians are called to recognize that astonishing fact. So we who journey with Jesus can share in his resurrection, which encompasses all people and pulls down all dividing walls.

In the life of the church the test is this: who would be the person whom you simply could not tolerate as part of the congregation. That is precisely the person Christ calls you accept, because Christ himself has died and been raised for her. The church can be on the front line of compassion, radical acceptance, and understanding.

This call to break barriers applies to us as individuals, too. In recent years I have become increasingly aware of how easily and quickly I discount people. I am sometimes an expert builder of barriers. When I reflect on my thoughts I am ashamed of myself. I dislike anyone who might make me look bad, anyone who reminds me of someone I dislike, people with tattoos, man with unpolished shoes, those who drive slowly on the interstate, and on and on. Apparently I love to divide, to wall off, to judge, to write off all sorts and conditions of persons.

I began wearing glasses in the third grade. I could for the first time see everything from the arithmetic problems on the black board to individual leaves on the trees. But several boys in the class taunted me with the title of "four eyes." To me it was obvious that it was not my fault that my eyes needed help, and I thought the title was stupid. Nevertheless, I longed for the name calling to disappear and to be accepted with or without glasses.

The name-calling was a small thing, but it had a hint of death about it, even for a seven year old. Nevertheless, I had been given a strong sense that God accepted me. It was resurrection for a little kid. Christ brings life and cuts down death in all its forms. Resurrection batters down barriers. The Risen Lord allows us to see others in light of his life and love. And the walls come tumbling down.

Eight, become a visionary. In John chapter twenty we have the wonderful story of the Risen Christ encountering Mary Magdalen in the garden on Easter morning. Mary had a limited, earth-bound view of matters: someone has stolen the body of Jesus. Then Jesus appears, broke down the barrier of her limited vision, and opened for her a new world. She now had become a visionary, a person who could imagine a world in which death was not the final word.

If death can be conquered by the deathless love of God, then the future belongs to Christ. The first chapter of Revelation calls Jesus the alpha and the omega, the beginning and the end, the whole alphabet. Jesus, in fact, *is* the future. This implies that the possibilities are huge, often beyond what we can imagine. Hence the writer of Ephesians can state that the God revealed in the resurrection "is able to accomplish abundantly far more than all we can ask or imagine" (Eph 3:20) At heart all Christians are visionaries, able to perceive the future in terms of the resurrection.

Over the years I have been involved in several capital fund drives to build or remodel church buildings. One issue always persists: how can people visualize what we are working for. Blueprints help a few, but most cannot make the mental transition from two dimensions to three. It's a matter of vision, being able to look beyond the printed page and see possibilities.

Barriers always do pop up. One is the tendency we all have to think that our plans and ideas are the best ones, if not the only ones. This can be called an overconfidence in one's self.

These are the "my way or the highway" people—and we all have a dose of it.

Moreover, people who have read the gospels can be guilty of dragging feet and limiting vision. They innately know that when you journey with Jesus he will upset the established order of things. Think of the story of the cleansing of the Temple in John's gospel. This was an attack on the whole sacrificial system that the Temple symbolized. I used to have a priest who often talked about "that pesky Jesus." Indeed!

And there is the matter of sin. Please understand that word as descriptive. It simply tells us about a constant fact about human beings. We all quickly and easily make the quiet assumption that we are the center of our own little universe. We think about ourselves all the time and we often work to take care of old number one. That defines sin. We have to struggle constantly to catch an alternative view of how our lives might be. We have a persistent creator-creature inversion at work in our hearts. The antidote, by the way, is worship, where we acclaim God as God and ourselves as not God.

How, then, do we move forward in a positive way to become resurrectionally visionary people? First, we should desire to be part of Jesus' resurrection movement. We need to discover that to love Jesus is to love the way he can open doors into the future. Ignatius Loyola often urges us to pray for the desire to love Jesus and be part of his mission, and if we cannot do that at least pray for the desire to desire.

A second step is to trust Christ to provide all that we need to do whatever grand project he calls us to. The assumption that we lack what we need, that we live with scarcity, betrays the resurrection. During high school, college, and seminary I worked at all sorts of jobs in order to help pay expenses. Never did I assume that my employer would not provide what I needed, and never did any employer assume that they did not have to supply basic tools. Why would we expect less from the one who loves us and gave himself for us?

To be a visionary assumes that we can catch a glimpse of God's vision. Thus, a third step is building up our ability to discern. This means waiting for the Risen Christ to open eyes of our heart to what he asks us to be and to do. In practice, we need to learn to be quiet and patient, neither of which is a common skill in our culture. We tend to be noisy people who seek quick answers, but this does not represent the normal way of divine activity. We need to be quiet enough for us to step out of the center of the picture so as to open a space for Christ. Patience works on the assumption that God works on divine time, not our time. Once we have gathered ourselves into a degree of patient calm we can then pray, search the scriptures, and seek the guidance of a spiritual director.

I recently visited our church camp, and one of the staff had brought with him his telescope of high quality. He and others told me about the night before when they had been able to see the rings of Saturn and some of the moons of Jupiter. But using a telescope requires darkness and a clear sky. Listening and watching for God's vision for our lives requires certain conditions: quiet, calm, scripture, prayer, and the guidance of other people of prayer.

A fourth step asks us to be willing to take a risk. Since we are speaking of God's vision, not our own, we can assume that we will be asked to step outside of our usual comfort zone. My experience tells me that walking with Jesus necessarily means that one will go to places which are unfamiliar and beyond our ability either to predict or control.

I often work with people who are trying to discern if Christ is calling them to the priesthood or the diaconate. Almost always an element of uncertainty is involved, as well as a struggle with what is asked of a person to be ordained. Priesthood, for example, requires pulling up roots, moving to a seminary, and finding a way to pay for it. I have never know a person called to holy orders who did not have to contend with fear about the enormous challenges that lay ahead. Nevertheless, they take the risk.

The last church I served faced a mission need, but dealing with it would unbalance the budget. The vestry and I talked about it for month. Finally they held their collective breathe and voted to proceed. My word to them was "congratulations."

God is the only true visionary. For the church and for individuals, Christ is the source of the dream of the whole world reconciled to God. Christ is the goal of the vision, and he is the source of the energy to pursue it.

In my office is a resurrection icon. It shows the Risen Christ dressed in blazing white kicking down the gates of hell and entering the domain of death. The doors lie shattered at his feet. With a cross held in his left hand, he reaches out to pull Adam and Eve from their graves. This icon represents the stunning vision of the victory of Christ over all the separates us from him; in Jesus the doors have been kicked down. This is the same Christ who declares his vision in these words: "Behold, I make all things news." (Rev. 21:5)

Nine, celebrate Eucharist. I remember a Christmas when I was in high school and had a perfectly miserable cold. I felt terrible and wanted only to go to bed and sleep. Despite that my parents pried me out of bed to help decorate the tree and to participate in some family events. So, how was I able to celebrate Christmas that year? Certainly not with a sense of joy and fun. But does that mean I did not celebrate Christmas because I did not experience the emotions associated with that holiday? The word "celebrate" has more to do with calling attention to and the lifting up of someone or something important rather than having a warm and cheery feeling. I did celebrate Christmas that year, not because I felt cheery but because I knew the story of the incarnation.

The word "Eucharist" is based on the Greek verb "to give thanks." Classic eucharistic prayers begin with a recital of reasons for giving thanks to God, and the climax of that list is always the death and resurrection of Christ. Thanksgiving stands at the heart of the lives of Christians. By giving thanks we begin to recognize God as the giver of every good and perfect gift, and from that point flows prayer, praise, generosity, and worship.

But Eucharist consist of more than that. We remember the death of Christ. This is not an act merely of recalling something. It is not like trying to remember where you placed the car keys. Remembrance in the Eucharist is when the past becomes present again. For example, when I look at my wedding ring, what comes to mind is much more than recalling the fact I was once involved in a marriage ceremony. It brings to mind my wife, our life together, and all the blessings that have flowed from relationship. That embodies the biblical sense of remembrance, and that is what happens in the Eucharist.

Eucharist also symbolizes the heavenly feast to come at the end of the age. Then we will be fully united with the Lord we love and will be transformed into his image. The Eucharist is the appetizer course of that banquet, in which we meet the Risen One in and under that bread and wine. So it always has that visionary, future-oriented nature.

Eucharist creates the community of the church. All the baptized share together in that event. We recognize and celebrate our common center in Christ. I am often taken aback when I kneel with others at the communion rail. Women and men, young and old, rich and poor, all presenting ourselves to Christ together, recognizing him as the one who gives life and love.

Eucharist, then, shapes and forms us. This becomes possible only because it is a resurrectional event, a holy time when we are encountered by the Risen Christ. For that moment we stand together in the new creation, that alternate reality of life and hope. And we leave changed, albeit often in imperceptible ways. Think of a string of Christmas tree lights. The bulbs hang dark and useless, until electric flows through the wire. Then they shine with light.

Eucharist is that time of resurrection when the electricity of Christ's life surges through us and among us, filling us with the light of life.

Eucharist stands at the very heart of our lives as the baptized. For Christians it forms the central act of our lives. It changes us, and little by little makes us new.

Some years back I was in Jerusalem, and on Sunday morning I decided to go to the Church of the Holy Sepulchre, the ancient church that stands on the sites of Jesus' death and resurrection. I arrived early enough that there were present only a few monks who tend the church. I made my way up the steps into the chapel atop Calvary. I simply lay prone on the floor before the altar and there gave to Christ the worries and pains of my life. Later I arose feeling liberated knowing that Jesus had taken my burdens on himself. Later I noticed that monks were setting up an altar at the entrance to the edicule, the structure that stands over Jesus' tomb. As Eucharist began the celebrant was standing inside the entrance to the edicule. After communion I found myself greeting those around me with the Easter declaration, Christ is risen, Christ is risen. That day I had entered more fully than ever before the reality of resurrection. Through the Eucharist that day, I was changed.

Ten, prepare for the paschal mystery. What I have in mind is that the pattern of the paschal mystery be so much of part of our thinking and imagination that we are able to observe the action of the Risen Lord in our lives. We would, then, be prepared to watch the movement from death to life happen before our eyes.

The mystery becomes imprinted on our hearts when we remember our baptism and when we witness the baptism of others. Watch the person go under the water and then be pulled out of it. That action denotes our union with the death and resurrection of our Lord. The liturgical action of Holy Week and Easter also imprint the mystery. At the Great Vigil of Easter, for example, we begin in darkness and move to the announcement of the resurrection, which is accompanied by bright lights, bells ringing, and organ fanfares.

At this point a warning may be necessary. The paschal mystery may unfold in ways that we did not want or expect. It may not be what we prayed for, and at the moment it may not seem to be new life. That simply means we need to keep the eyes of our heart open as the mystery unfolds some more. For example, I have known people who were devastated by the loss of their jobs, but later were able to sense that that trauma had been taken in the life of the Risen Lord and that something good had come from it.

In the icon tradition of Orthodox Christianity, there are two official images for Easter. I have described one above in which Christ has broken the gates of hell. The second and more common is entitled "The Myrrh Bearers." On the left of the icon two of the women who had witnessed Jesus' death are returning to his tomb both carrying vessels of myrrh with which to anoint the body. They clutch the vessels closely and grief is written across their faces. They signify all of us bearing our pains and perplexities on our way to the cemetery. At the center of the icon sits a huge angel clothed in white with wings of gold. He looks at the women while pointing with his right hand to a dark cave on the right side of the icon. In the cave is a coffin containing burial clothes but nothing else. No corpse. No body. The angel is the agent of the paschal mystery pointing to the cave—which contains nothing. No death. No decay. Do we not live in that icon? All we have left for us is to recognize that the tomb contains nothing at all.

Easter questions for discussion:

First, what is the most significant learning about living with the Risen Lord that you take from this chapter?

Two, what barriers do you see in yourself and in the church that stand in the way of living in the resurrection?

Third, which of the ten commandments of resurrectional living helped you most? Which one caused you the most trouble?

Fourth, as you journey with Jesus in living the paschal mystery what spiritual discipline do you need most to develop?

Finally, if you had occasion to tell a friend about what resurrection means to you what would you say?

A Final Word

I CAN STILL REMEMBER my family's first vacation. I was probably four or five years old, and we have gone to the beach. I recall picking up smooth rocks, wading in cold water, and drinking my first cup of hot tea. And I can recollect the sad feeling of leaving, going home, and finishing that special time.

We come to the end of our time together making this journey with Jesus. But I hope that nothing sad enters your heart and mind. Rather I pray that this marks the beginning of a new and revitalized pilgrimage with Jesus. My aim has been to help you know and love him in a new and more profound way.

In our time together I have often referred to material from Luke and Acts. Almost certainly they were written by the same person so that one can properly read them as one book with two parts. It begins with the writer saying that he has "undertaken to set down an orderly account of the events that have been fulfilled among us." (Lk 1:1) Then he unfolds the story of Jesus from birth to death to resurrection and to ascension. As Jesus departs this dimension he charges the apostles to wait for the arrival of the Holy Spirit. That serves as the transition to the book of Acts, which reports the beginning of the church focusing especially on the apostles Peter and Paul. But the story does not so much end as it simply stops. We are told that Paul is in prison in Rome, but that he is free to teach. And there the story stops. I believe this is intentional. It is as if the writer is saying to us readers: now the story continues in you; it's your time to follow Jesus and live in the power of his resurrection. I hope you have reached the point where you can take up that challenge.

My desire is that we can say together the prayer of St. Richard of Chichester together. "Day by day, dear Lord, of thee three things I pray: to see thee more clearly, love thee more dearly, follow thee more nearly, day by day."